COPYRIGHT ©SAPN

All rights reserved. No part of this publication may be reproduced, stored in a retrieval system, or transmitted in any form or by any means, electronic, mechanical, photocopying, recording or otherwise, without the publisher's prior written permission.

First Impression 2024

This book is sold subject to the condition that it shall not, by trade or otherwise, be lent, resold, hired out or otherwise circulated without the publisher's prior permission in any form of binding or cover other than in which it is published.

The views expressed in this book are entirely those of the author.

All disputes are subject to arbitration, and legal actions, if any, are subject to the jurisdiction of courts in New Delhi, India.

Dear Reader,

I am blessed to have you reading this.
Of what use is the shade of a tree,
If no traveller rests beneath it?
Of what use is the flower's fragrance,
If no one ever delights in it?
For whatever exists here and now,
It is enriched by benefitting one another.
Such are these lines of mine,
Kindles love and faith in reading and writing.

Email: contactme.sapnadeb@gmail.com
Website: www.sapnadeb.com

INTRODUCTION

I have been a nature lover for as long as I can remember. The sun, the moon, the stars, the rain and the wind, the chirp and the chuckle, the whispers and the howls, the croaks and the laughs, the fluttering and swishing—I have seen and heard them all.

I lived where large open spaces of land lay bare, inviting with open arms. You could see as far as your eyes could see. As I watched, mesmerised on the distant horizon, the creator unleashed his new piece of art in the early evening every day. The mighty sun dipped in the confluence of the earth and the sky. The twilight sky blazed a deep orange, light orange, purple, pink, grey and black with streaks of gold in rapid succession. I know not when, in a sacred moment, I became one with them.

As night fell, I saw a few trees come alive and open their unseen eyes while the others fell asleep. At other times, I had glimpses of the unifying thread that runs through all living beings.

My life is rich with varied experiences in the hills, where I have lived for more than twenty-four years. The timeless hills have strange secrets hidden in their bosom.
Sometimes, they whisper, and sometimes, they have a strange power that permeates those who walk on their furtive trails or breathe in their crisp air.
The power to be content and happy while leading an austere life. The power to share the only morsel of food one has.

The hills vibrate with spectacular energy. Do the living saints have something to do with it?

This collection is the sequel to my book**, And They Survived**. It is a collection of personal anecdotes and experiences of mine or those near me. All of them are based on truth. Some offer a rare glimpse into a world that exists here and now, hanging beyond a veil—the veil that sometimes dissolves for me.

I have been writing about my experiences for a long time. You can read about them in my books **How to Boost Self-Esteem, How To Create Positive Emotions, and How to Transform Negative Emotions**.

    Most of them have brought smiles or tears at times but have been rewarding, for along the way, they have helped shape my character and destiny and made my life unique.

Writing this collection has been a rewarding experience, for nothing gives me more happiness than this.

COPYRIGHT SAPNA DEB 2024

INTRODUCTION

CHAPTER 1	1
WHISPERS AT NIGHT	1
CHAPTER 2	15
TO ERR IS HUMAN	15
CHAPTER 3	19
SUBTERFUGE	19
CHAPTER 4	28
TWO SISTERS	28
CHAPTER 5	34
THE DOG'S GRACE	34
CHAPTER 6	38
LIFE GOES ON	38
CHAPTER 7	48

THE LITTLE GHOST	48
CHAPTER 8	**53**
MY ENGLISH TEACHER	53
CHAPTER 9	**57**
UNSEEN WORLD	57
CHAPTER 10	**64**
CRIES OF REGRET	64
CHAPTER 11	**74**
MY MISER UNCLE	74
CHAPTER 12	**79**
THE HOODED MAN	79
CHAPTER 13	**90**
SOJOURN INTO THE PAST	90
CHAPTER 14	**97**
NOCTURNAL ADVENTURES	97

CHAPTER 15	103
I SLIPPED TO MY DEATH	103
REVIEW REQUEST	112
OTHER BOOKS BY THE AUTHOR	113
DEDICATION	114
ACKNOWLEDGEMENT	115
AFTERWORD	129

Chapter 1

Whispers at Night

Steam rose in tiny ringlets from my cup of tea. I watched them, fascinated. She also watched me. I felt ill at ease under her gaze, for she did not merely look at me. The depths of my soul had been suddenly struck bare. Her cloudy eyes were watching that in grave suspicion.

I shifted uncomfortably in my chair. This was too unsettling. As I got up to leave, the cloudy eyes cleared and sparkled.
"You cannot leave like this. At least finish your tea and the biscuits. I don't think I have given you too many tasks over the weekend. You cannot be in a hurry," she said.
She would know. Dr. Anamika was the Registrar of the Ophthalmology unit, where I had joined for a two-month fellowship training. I was entirely at her mercy.

I resumed my place. The compact room had a bed that was too narrow for her, a table, an almirah, and a small fridge. The walls were decorated with little paper butterflies, stickers of fruits and vegetables, and three dark, strange faces. Their eyes were dark and deep, and they seemed to stare at me.

My imagination was running wild. I should concentrate on my cup instead of letting my eyes roam. A sudden tremor ran down my spine. Her eyes had gone dark and were burning into me.
The look changed as our eyes met, and she broke into a smile. The smile, though, could not dissolve the guarded look in her eyes.
"Do you like those faces? Are they not interesting?" She asked.
"Yes, they are interesting and scary, too," I muttered.

She laughed, and I joined in. The abrupt ease in the tension made me feel brave. I munched the biscuits.

"I feel very bored and lonely. My husband is in another city in a distant part of this country. I have been married for five years. I even had a child, but he died at birth," she said, as a look of pain crossed her face.
I listened in silence.
"I remained sick for a long time. Once I recovered, I wanted to continue my studies. My temperament also changed after that sickness. We were a loving couple earlier but later started having frequent fights," she said.
"How is your husband? You are married too, aren't you? Does he take proper care of you?" She asked.
"He is good," I answered.
"That does not mean that my husband does not care for me. He sends me money every month. How else do you think I can afford this excellent food? Our institute pays us peanuts for this eighteen—to twenty-hour daily work schedule. I can only afford this room and two paltry meals a day. We are worse than menial labourers," she said with a bitter laugh.

I agreed with her. At least this institute gave them peanuts. There were other galore which only allowed learning to postgraduate doctors for similar hours. They dare not protest; they would be shown the door the next day. I was fortunate, for I had gone to study there after securing a government delegation. My salary would be credited to my account during that period, too. It was a blessing.

I had wanted to do a two-year fellowship similar to hers. But how long could I ask my parents to shoulder my burden? Some dreams remain

3

uncertain and never see the light of day. One can sigh remembering them.

A sudden movement caught my eye. Dr Anamika had almost leapt up from her sitting position and removed multiple packets from the fridge. Despite her heavy countenance, she was agile. Her movement was startling. It seemed like a smooth glide of a bat, but I saw wolves in my mind's eye.
She opened each packet one by one and ate them hungrily. Packets of burgers, chips, different kinds of cheese, and cookies were emptied rapidly.
"Do not mind my eating in this manner. I have a robust appetite," she said sheepishly.

I understood her predicament. The food served in the canteen was so disagreeable that many resident doctors ate none. I developed a liking for curds and made my unique dish by adding rice, salad, and pickles. This had become my daily diet.
We discussed other mundane things, and then the conversation again veered towards my personal life.
"Are you happy with your marriage?" She asked.
I replied in the affirmative.
"Well, I was happy too earlier. Shubhas and I gelled well, but then things changed over time. Does love fade away slowly? The death of our son disappointed me. I bled profusely for days. The doctors wanted to remove my uterus to save me. We did not want that. I held on for dear life. Within a month, I became so weak that I could hardly get up from my bed. I prayed fervently to God during those days. Now, I have stopped," she said with resignation.

I felt sad listening to her but did not know how to console her. Besides that, a strange invisible veil seemed to be hanging between us. I seemed to guard

4

against something hostile at a subconscious level. It disconcerted me further because, try as I may, I could not put my finger on it.

"You can see a few things, isn't it?" She turned her search light-like glowing eyes into me.
My heart almost stopped beating.
"What do you mean?" I asked, trying to speak as calmly as I could.
"You know what I mean. Things invisible to others are discernible to you...like GHOSTS," she said, watching me.
My heart did a sudden somersault. This secret had always lay hidden in the deepest recesses within me. How could it become so apparent to a perfect stranger? Perhaps my thoughts were mirrored on my face. One side of her mouth twisted into a sly, triumphant smile, and then she looked anxious.
"Tell me all about it," she said.
It was not a request.
"I saw a few strange things in my childhood, and that is all," I said evasively.

"Please tell me. I am very interested in these things. Do you believe in past lives? Have you heard of reincarnation?" She asked.
"I am not sure about these things but have heard about it," I said.
"I believe in reincarnation without a shadow of doubt. There is a reason behind it," she said.
My interest was kindled. Leaning towards her, I waited in anticipation.

"Mohan was our neighbour. Shyam was his childhood friend. Mohan's father was a wealthy businessman. Shyam's father was a tailor. Since they studied in the same school, they became acquainted.

This acquaintance blossomed into a strong friendship. Shyam was a cheerful and decent boy, and Mohan's father was fond of him too. Both continued their studies further in different institutions. Mohan studied engineering while Shyam pursued commerce and slowly grew apart. Mohan started a small leather industry after graduation, and within a few years, it became very successful. He bought a new sprawling bungalow and moved away from our locality. After some time, Shyam also joined his industry. Mohan was overjoyed to be with his friend again and offered him a partnership in his company.

A few years later, Mohan went overseas for company-related work. It took longer than expected. On his return, he got the rudest shock of his life. His company and bungalow had become Shyam's sole property. The 'power of attorney' given to the latter had become his Waterloo. Mohan could not survive the shocking betrayal. He died soon after.

Shyam's company attained dizzying heights. He married a beautiful lady, Suman. Their son was born after two years. Arvind was a chubby and naughty little boy. All doted on him. One day, he fell ill and was admitted to a nearby hospital. He remained there for days but did not get well. His parents took him from one reputed hospital to another in most of the country's major cities, but his health worsened. He had a rare type of leukaemia.

They had to sell the bungalow and, in due course, their company to pay for the mounting hospital bills. Arvind stayed semi-conscious in his bed for months, with his eyes closed, hanging between the realm of life and death. His parents sat beside him, grieving.

One night, he suddenly opened his eyes and gazed at them. His parents were joyous with relief.
"Oh God! Thank you so much," Suman said, holding his hands between hers.
Tears of joy ran down Shyam's eyes. He bent down to kiss his forehead.
"Father, you have not recognised me," Arvind whispered.
"What do you mean, my dear child?" Shyam said, surprised.
"I am not your son. I am Mohan. Today, you have lost everything you ever owned. You neither have the company nor the bungalow. My revenge is complete," he said and closed his eyes forever."

A stunned silence filled the room.
"Our bad deeds return to haunt us in one way or another. This is an extreme example of it," she said after some time.
"Yes, what an unbelievable story! I hope I have harmed no one during my life," I said.
I had broken the ice.

"I wish I could always be healthy. The time after my child's death was the worst phase of my life. I had become so weak that I could not even sit up. My husband was busy with his patients. My dreams were filled with nightmares. Strange demons attacked me and stayed on. I thought I would perish, but somehow, I survived all that," she said after some time.
My heart went out to her.
"Do not worry. God will always keep you well," I said.
"Do you think so? Please look at me. Do you see something in me?" She asked.

"What can I probably see in you?" I asked, perplexed.

She evaded the question and then started talking about our other teachers. I wanted to leave, but she held me with her constant talking.
"Are you sure that you see nothing of consequence in me?" She asked again after some time.
I assured her that I found her all right.
"You do not understand my question," she said with a troubled voice.
Rubbing her hands together in desperation, she deliberated her next move. By then, I had almost reached the door. She did not want me to leave.
"DO YOU SEE A GHOST IN ME?" She stood up, asking me haltingly.

I stopped in my tracks, stunned. Her fair face bore anxiety, exasperation, expectation, and eagerness. My heart was filled with warmth for her.
"How can you be a Ghost?" I smiled, saying that.
"Are you sure that I have no ghost within me? You can see them, can't you?" She persisted.
"Yes, I can see them, but you are fine, and I see nothing in you," I said with a finality in my voice and left her room.
She avoided my gaze, but her apparent discontent and dissent were evident.

I had never met a stranger lady, and the whole evening had been wasted with no gain in my knowledge of Ophthalmology. I decided that henceforth, I would decline every invitation from any quarter.

The next day, I met her in the clinical room, smiling as ever, and my heart sighed in relief. A month passed away, and I had another month of training left. We worked hard all day, went to the library, pondered over small, printed journals, and tried to remember the lines written in multiple volumes of books, and my study hours extended up to the wee hours of the morning.

All the girls in the adjacent rooms would be asleep. Their sleeping for long hours filled me with pity for myself. I closed the door at about 11 p.m. every night, ensuring I would not need to get out again. The row of washrooms was at the farthest end of the long corridor. Next to it was an extensive area with basins on either side and an extended washing area with a row of taps on the opposite end. The girls washed their utensils and clothes there. Large windows opened on either side near the basins, with enormous trees peering inside. The light filtering in from posts along the yonder roads and the swaying branches of trees threw dancing ominous shadows on the floor. The wind made strange sounds as it whistled playfully through the leaves while the owls howled. It didn't seem very safe. So, I avoided going there at night.

I had noticed a very peculiar thing from the last couple of nights. At about 2 a.m. every night, I heard a door click open softly, and then 'someone' moved in the corridor towards the washroom. There was no sound of footsteps, even in the dead of the night. I also felt the person standing for some time outside my door before moving on. My table was about two feet away, and a sudden terror arose within me when 'It' did so. I could almost feel the presence of that 'someone.' A strange, chilling, barely audible, and continuous SHhhhhhhhhhhh... sound accompanied it.

When I felt 'It' receding away, I would switch off the lights and cover myself from head to toe. My heart would continue to beat wildly and calm down after some time. Sleep would steal over me then.

How long could I sustain this? Only two weeks remained of my training, and I had a lot of reading to do. I noticed that 'someone' returned at around three a.m. My heart always started dancing when it came near, and I heard a very clear "Shhhhh" sound when it did so. It always waited for some time outside my door. I felt like 'it' was watching me, though a thick wooden door separated us.

Slowly, I started feeling ashamed of my cowardice. I decided I would conquer my fear by coming face to face with it. One night, I waited with bated breath. The clock struck two a.m. There was a soft click of the door and then silence. Strangely, 'It' did not wait upon my door. I peeped outside from a slit-like opening of the door. Light filtered outside, and I saw Dr Anamika walking away, dangling a bucket and mug in her hands! Almost gasping loudly in surprise, I closed the door immediately, soundlessly.

After ten minutes, I removed my slippers and tiptoed towards the washing area. The corridor was dimly lit because of the stray rays of a solitary bulb shining outside one of the washrooms. I passed about ten rooms on either side. All were still and plunged in darkness. My heart was jumping inside me. I hoped against hope that 'It' would be the 'same one' who waited by my door every night. It had not done so that night.

It was then that the sound hit me in full force. SHhhhhhh…................... I realised that I was not hearing it with my human ear. Something else within me heard that. The splashing sound of water suddenly stopped. The door remained closed, but 'It' started gazing at me with wild anger as the Door suddenly dissolved—absolute terror filled my being.

'RUN…RUN…. RUN WITH ALL YOUR MIGHT…' Voices screamed inside me. (My Guardian angels were warning me.) My hands and feet trembled, but I could not move. I remained rooted at the spot while staring at the door in absolute horror.
'YOU HAVE COME TO SPY ON ME!' I heard 'It' say with ferocious anger clearly.
I remained standing there, paralysed and filled with a deep sense of impending doom. There was no escape!

Suddenly, 'someone' took over my body, and everything blurred. I was transported to my room. (My angels were helping me.)
   I could latch the door with great difficulty, for my hands were shaking with fright, and my teeth were chattering. 'It' was in my hot pursuit. I jumped into bed, shaking and praying to Shiva and Kali Ma. I had barely covered my head when 'It' reached my door but did not stop there. It directly came in as the SHhhhhhhhhhhh…. blared into my ears. An ominous shadow stood by my bedside.

"So, you are following me! You dare to follow me!" 'It' said, in violent anger.
"I am sorry and will never do so again. Please forgive me!" I mumbled repeatedly.
My head was covered with the quilt, but I still could feel 'It' standing beside me.

"Save me... save me... save me...save me..." I prayed fervently to Shiva.
I drifted away to sleep once it went away after what seemed an 'eternity' in time.

The following day, I reached the hospital a little later than usual. I felt tired and listless, and the scare and lack of adequate sleep of yesterday showed. Dr Anamika looked at me with disdain and lapsed into total silence. It was understandable. She had a vehement dislike for latecomers.
My eyes invariably turned to her again and again. I could neither believe the incident from earlier that night nor the fresh looks on her face. This is an illusionary world.

We had to wait all day at the operation theatre to watch the operations being done. The television screens displayed the operations live. I had been standing for almost ten hours. My feet were giving away. I collapsed on the only chair there. It was not for me but for our teachers.
I got up with a start after some time. Professor Sharma stood opposite me, frowning.
"I'm sorry, Sir. May I please go back early today? I can't stand here," I muttered.
"What has happened to the junior doctors of today? They cannot even... Oh! You look very pale. Please go back to the hostel and rest," he said with alarm.
He sent a friend of mine, Dr Vijaya, to accompany me back.
"Pack some food from the canteen for her," he told her.

Vijaya stayed with me, talking and caring for me. My body was burning with a high fever. It refused to come down despite medicines. I had to be admitted to one ward in the hospital. I could neither eat nor sleep. Multiple tubes remained wired to me. This continued for a week. Since there were no signs of recovery, the Institute Director ordered me to go home.

I was taken aback. How could he do so? My home was far away, and I would have to change flights once in between. I was progressively getting weaker and could hardly sit up without help. Embarking on a journey back home alone was unfathomable. My mother was tending to my ailing father then, so she could not come to take me back. My husband was away in another country. I was in a dilemma. I continued to be in the hospital until the next day's air tickets were handed to me.

There was no other way except to leave. I hated the unkind Director. He had virtually thrown me off the hostel and the Institute. Many Professors there disapproved of his behaviour. They requested that he let me stay on until I recovered a little. But he would hear of no such thing.

A five-hour taxi drive would take me to the nearest airport. Tired, weak, and suffering from jaundice and typhoid, I embarked on a lengthy road journey. Surprisingly, the further I moved away from the town, the better I felt. A 'shadow' seemed to lift off me as I went farther away. When I reached the airport, I felt almost as healthy and cheerful as usual! I looked forward eagerly to my onward journey.

As the plane lifted itself, I felt my spirit soar. After some time, my tired eyes seemed to close on their own. Suddenly, Dr. Anamika's image flashed clearly into my mind's eye.

"I was so weak that I could not even sit up. My dreams were filled with nightmares. Strange demons attacked and stayed on....," she was saying.

The stark truth dawned on me then. I almost jumped up in my seat. My body was being prepared for 'It's' final 'grand entry'! It had become so weak that I could barely sit up straight. I had been saved by the skin of my teeth!

My heart bowed in reverence to our Director. I was angry at his unsympathetic behaviour. He had neither let me return to the hostel nor allowed me to continue staying in the ward there. He had sent me packing by sending the air tickets and, in the process, had stopped making another Dr Anamika midway.
God works through his angels in this world. 'Be not forgetful to entertain strangers: for thereby some have entertained angels unawares.' Hebrews 13.2.

"Oh God, be with her as you have been with me. Be with her, my God." I prayed silently as tears ran down my eyes.

CHAPTER 2

TO ERR IS HUMAN

"Doctor, please come soon. One of the patients is no longer responding. We have tried everything but failed to revive him," the nurse was telling me.

I was filling out the forms for a medicolegal patient in the casualty department then. I left it midway and started towards the medicine ward.

A small skeleton-like man lay on the bed motionless. His face and mouth were covered with oozing ulcers. I checked the eyes and examined for heart and breath sounds. His eyes remained wide open, staring at the ceiling.
"He is dead," I signalled to the nurse.
"Where are the relatives?" I asked her.
She pointed outside.

Three teenage boys were waiting outside, trifling with their mobiles. I told them as gently as I could. Waves of relief spread across their faces.
"Can we take him now?" One asked eagerly.
I was amazed at the indifference.

"Is he your father?" I asked.
"No, we are neighbours," one of them replied.
"Does he not have a wife, children, or anyone else in his family?" I asked.
"He has them, doctor," another boy said.
"Do they know he is here?" I asked, amazed.
"Yes, they do. They stay nearby. But they do not want to come here to visit him," he replied.

I was at a loss for words.
The nurse was gesturing at me wildly.
"Doctor, come in soon," she said.
I went in.

"Doctor, see, the dead patient is crying!" She pointed at him.

A few drops seemed to be trickling from the corners of his eyes, which had a faraway look. I closed his eyes and wiped out the tears. I rechecked the heart. There was no sound.

I thought of filling out the death certificate. On impulse, I touched the chest with the stethoscope again. I thought I heard a faint beat, but it disappeared, and then there was a fresh trickle of tears. I was at a loss. Was he dead, or only looked so? Suddenly, I was not very sure.

"I think he is alive. I cannot fill this form now," I said.

We made another effort to revive him but failed.
My heart was filled with dismay. He did not want to die just then. He was fighting. He was waiting for someone. Time was running out for him. I could sense the intense despair, the intense longing...

"Call his wife and children. Don't they realise they have to be here?" I said.
"What can we do?" One of them said.
"Do you have their phone number?" I asked.
He nodded.
"Then call them now. Tell them to come over immediately," I said.

The sister in charge was beckoning me.
"They will not come. I know them. He never took care of his family when he could. He spent all his money on alcohol and womanising. That is how he developed this immunodeficiency, too. They have nothing to do with him anymore," she said calmly.

I was at an absolute loss of words.

"You are required in the casualty now. We will take care of it until then," she added.

I retraced my steps back slowly. Life was fleeting. He had lived without care for one's own. Why did he seek them now in his final moments?

I thought of his wife and kids. Was it so difficult to forgive a dying man who was extending his hands towards them? Had he not suffered enough already? But, of course, I knew little of their side of the story. They say death is a great leveller. It wipes out suffering and pain. But can it restore peace in broken hearts? Only time will tell...

CHAPTER 3

SUBTERFUGE

I was a Junior resident in the Ophthalmology department at that time. Dr. Beena was my co-resident. We shared the same room, and our tables stood at opposite corners.

Next to our room was the room of Dr Seema, one of our lecturers. Dr Rawat, the other lecturer, occupied the next room. The last room of the row belonged to two other residents, Dr Nimish and Dr Chandrasekhar.

The infrastructure was excellent and unbroken, i.e., the chairs and tables looked respectable. Ours were on the verge of collapsing. I always needed help understanding the guys. They always got the best of everything. Their means to it were beyond our comprehension.

Since we were merely students, we were at a loss with many of the patients. If any of them gave distress signals to our brains, we trotted over to Seema Madam's room with our patients. She was our favourite and would explain to us softly. A rare beauty with brains, she was sweet-tempered, too.

We went to Dr Rawat only if she was too busy. On such days, we went timidly to him. His unpredictable temper always made us a little jittery. It erupted like a dormant volcano with no warning. After meeting him when we would return, each of us would have realised our 'moronic' status of existence. At other times, he was as good as gold and had a wonderful sense of humour. His round goblet eyes would do the acting to accompany his talking, and I would go into raptures witnessing the performance.

We were all in awe of the Department head, Dr. Ram. He was a towering gentleman in terms of height and knowledge. We felt like pygmies in his presence. His room was at the farthest end of the Department, adjoining the office. We went to him with patients worth being presented in the clinical meetings.

The patient rush did not seem to ebb that day. They crowded all over us, breathing down our necks. Even after repeated requests, they did not make a line. We felt claustrophobic and suffocated. I longed for the patient line to end. After four hours, we asked for tea for a much-needed break. We were about to resume when Dr Rawat entered the room.

"Tanu, you come to my room right now. There is a patient who wishes to be seen only by Your Highness," he said, stamping his feet.
I stood up hurriedly, perplexed beyond measure.
"I am a lecturer and your teacher. When I am ready to see him, he refuses and wants you instead," he continued in disgust.
Beena gave me an incredible look. I quietly followed him to his room.

An old, weary man wearing dirty, tattered clothes was brooding in the patient's chair. His face brightened upon seeing me.
"Oh Tanu, my dear child! I am so happy to see you!" He said with relief.

To say I was aghast was to put it mildly. How did beggars know my first name? In some instances, I had contributed to their begging bowls, but I needed to remember when I had formally introduced myself to one.
"You did not recognise me," he said sadly.

I tried to recall the faces of beggars within a five-kilometre radius of the Hostel. My memory ultimately failed me. All had old, wrinkled faces. That's all I had noted.

I remembered Dr. Ram's repeated discourses on being more observant and dwelling in the present than in the past or future.

"Do not stand there and dream! You do not know this person, but he knows you by name. This is what I understand. Is my conclusion correct?" Dr. Rawat's voice boomed again.
"It is not the child's fault," the man said.
"It's me who has become like this," he continued.
"Tanu, do you remember your Sukhwinder Uncle?" He asked further.
An instant wave of recognition swept over me.

"Oh, Uncle! Is it you? Sorry, I did not recognise you. What happened to you suddenly?" I said, hardly able to hide my intense surprise.
"That is a long story. I have come here to get my eyes operated on, and I place myself in your hands completely," he said with folded hands.
I heard a snort from Dr Rawat.

"She will operate on you! She has not even started learning to do that. Are you out of your mind?" He asked.
That made him more adamant and Dr Rawat angrier.
"I will not let any other doctor touch my eyes," Mr. Sukhwinder said.
Dr Rawat immediately ordered me to leave his room along with him.

I took him outside but could not find a place to make him seated.

I whispered in his ears, "Do not insist on me to be your surgeon. I have not yet started learning to do surgeries. He is a good surgeon. Let him operate on you."

He reluctantly agreed. I peeped into Dr Rawat's room. He still looked angry. His already big eyes looked bigger and red. This was not the opportune time to seek a countenance.

I told Uncle to come again after two days. He groaned in resignation and walked away slowly with his wife. There was so much melancholy and grief in his demeanour that I felt miserable. I went back quietly to my room. Patients were a little less then.

Unlike other days, I could see Beena's face as she spoke, "One-to-one contact with a beggar, right from childhood. Well... well... It can be possible only with you. I am not surprised a bit."

A sigh escaped me. I continued attending to my many patients. The attendant came, thrust a big bundle of outpatient slips on my table and another on the other, and left. It was 2 p.m. already. My stomach was growling, and so were the patients', probably. At least I was seated in a chair, though I could do with some air. They had been standing for long hours, patiently awaiting their turn.

Our rooms, though big, had two small windows. Black paper was stuck on them, and they were kept closed to keep the light out. We needed darkness to facilitate eye examinations and other diagnostic procedures. This darkness seemed to be seeping into me.

Someday, when I become a woman of substance, I will make a nice room for myself. Its big windows would allow fresh air to flow in. Small potted plants would be my companion there. A polite attendant would make the patients wait in line and send them individually. They would not flow into my room like a flood, drowning me.

"What a frivolous idea!" Beena exclaimed suddenly. I nearly jumped out of my skin.

"What are you sitting and dreaming about? Fresh air. We won't get all this soon. So stop your silly dreams!" She said.

I was sure my head was transparent so everyone could read my thoughts to the minute detail. My future was in jeopardy.
"Come on now. Do not sit and think about the how. Finish examining your patients fast. I am as hungry as you are for food and fresh air," she added.

I went back to my work. By the time we finished, it was past 4.40 p.m.

On returning to the hostel, I kept thinking of Mr. Sukhwinder. He was the wealthiest man in our colony and had over a hundred trucks, which he used for his coal transportation business. He also had a heart of gold and helped everyone in need. Many people he helped monetarily start their businesses had become millionaires.

Children were his favourite. His pockets were full of exotic chocolates, which he used to bring back from his world tours, especially for us. He also had a fleet of cars we loved to ride in. I remembered the Maruti car he had bought when it was newly launched in India. When I sat in that toy car the first time, I wished fervently to take my hand out and touch the long ribbon-like fast disappearing road, for it seemed so near.

His wife was a kind lady. She made delicacies in enormous quantities for distribution. It seemed like a house where perennial parties were held for all. One could walk in and help himself to whatever one needed. He had houses in many cities but preferred staying in a government residential quarter because of his love for everyone there.

A large family lived next to him. The father was a peon and found it difficult to feed all seven children with that meagre salary. Mr Sukhwinder was a boon to them. One of the children, a boy named Dilshan, had become my classmate in class five after failing thrice in different courses. Uncle took him under his wing since he was not inclined to study further after class seven. He taught and tutored him about the basics of business. Since God never gave him one, he thought of him as his child. Dilshan's life turned over entirely after that.

I sometimes wondered at this, for I never could see any good in that boy. He was a bully and a rogue, but Mr. Sukhwinder saw potential in him. He loved him, and Dilshan turned over a new leaf under his care and guidance. Slowly, he put a significant part of his business in his hands to monitor his work and give help and advice. All was well when I last saw him over twelve years back.

They came two days after that. I took them to the doctor's room in the eye ward. The tale that unfolded was a staggering one of cruelty and deceit. It was as if someone had pulled the ground off from below my feet.

Dilshan slowly took over everything, from the businesses and houses in different parts of the country to almost everything he had. They now stayed in a small room in his mansion, literally starving. Food was provided once a day in inadequate quantity. Armed guards guarded their room outside. They had no money and were given only ten rupees for the day here. This being inadequate for the bus fare, they walked for three hours to the hospital. It filled me with anger.
"I will report it to the police," I said.
He joined his hands and pleaded, "Please do not do so. He will kill us then. He is powerful and can get away with anything."

I knew not what to say.
"It is my fate," he said in resignation.
I searched in my pockets.
"Please accept this," I said, offering a hundred rupee note.
"No... ... we can't accept this from our daughter," both said together.
I requested them again and again, but they declined.

I brought some snacks for them, which they kindly accepted. After leaving them there, I went to Dr. Rawat to request the operation date.

The operation, done a week later, was uneventful, and he returned happily, blessing me as always.

I remembered the hundreds of people whom he had helped throughout his life. Could they not join hands together to help him? Some of them had shifted to Canada. Once the work of the ladder is over, it is thrown off unceremoniously.

I fervently wished I could help them. They did not want to accept any money from me. I was a hosteller surviving on a meagre stipend. There was no place where I could keep them.

Mr Sukhwinder had given Dilshan his all. Because of him, he was in a state of affluence and grandeur. His foray into the world of luxury had taken off from the latter's grounds. I prayed that he would return someday to that same holy ground. But it was not to be.

Mr. Sukhwinder and his wife eventually embraced death in quiet resignation to deception by a loved one.

CHAPTER 4

TWO SISTERS

"One of you can sit here in front of me. The other one can sit here beside me. Settle yourself comfortably. Now close your left eye and read what you can see in the mirror opposite to you with your right eye. Try your best. There is no need to try to excel by looking through the space between your fingers with the supposedly closed eye. There is no need to impress me," I repeated like a parrot to my next patient, an old, upright lady with a face lined with happy-looking wrinkles.

She nodded and seated herself.
"You can read A, B, C, and D, right?" I asked.
Another nod. A lady of few words. Quite rare, I thought to myself and smiled.
She peered at the mirror with slit-like eyes.

"Try to read what you see," I said encouragingly.
She started, her voice quivering, "M …"
"There is no M there. Try again," I said.
"U…aaa," She spluttered.

"You forgot your ABCs! My God! What will you do next?" the younger sister asked, laughing loudly.
"No, I haven't. It is just that the words on the mirror are too small," the older one, Elisha, protested.
"It's alright. Keep trying," I assured her.

The more Elisha tried reading and failed, the more Melisha laughed. I thought she would fall off the chair and break a few old bones.
"You are growing older by the day. You have lost your memory!" She added, tears of mirth flowing out from her eyes.

Elisha looked embarrassed and smiled self-consciously. I was at a loss for words. I was enjoying the scene and smiling within. Laughter is contagious, like a yawn.

"It is alright. You will see with glasses," I assured her. I examined her and saw that she did not have cataracts. Her eyes were perfect for her age. Shortly after that, I handed over her prescription.

It was Melisha's turn then. She was of medium height and light brown complexion and confidently stood tall. She sat on the chair next to me and closed one eye. A sudden trepidation ran through her. She gave me a look of shock and turned towards the mirror again.

By then, Elisha had placed herself right opposite me and had rested her elbows at the edge of my table. She watched Melisha with great interest, a wicked smile on her lips.

"What happened, my dear young lady? Read for your honour's sake!" She ordered.
 Melisha looked confused and embarrassed. She made her eye progressively smaller.
"No, no, that will not do. No need to turn into a Chinese woman!" Elisha roared.
I broke into a loud laughter, and so did we all.

"Don't you see she is making her eyes look like the Chinese, doctor?" Asked Elisha.
I nodded.
"Leave her alone! Let her try at least," I told her imploringly.
Melisha tried in vain, "Ah…umm…"

By then, Elisha had jumped up with delight and blurted out, "There you are, oldie! You can't remember a single alphabet! At least I had read an M, but you can't even read that."
"Please, there is no M...." I started but stopped.
I was loving every moment of it.

"Madam, we have not touched our books in fifty years. Once we do some schooling and get married, books serve no purpose. Though she is younger than me, I know she is getting older by her ways. She cannot catch a fish these days," she said dismissively.

Probably the smaller ones swish out from her hands, or the net was not thrown at the most lucrative spot. Reflexes do get slower over time, I thought to myself.

"Next time when you go fishing, carry your glasses with you. You will see the little fish better and each other," I told them.
They broke into a hearty laugh.

"We only have each other. We married and bore children. Our husbands died. The children went out of the village to study and then work. They will never return. Nowadays, no one wants to stay in the village," the older sister said sadly.

"I explain to them that we grow vegetables, rear poultry, and catch fresh fish from the streams. Our grounds are laden with fruit trees. We breathe fresh air. Where do the kids go to exercise these days? Gym...Our village pathways and the nearby forests are our gyms," Melisha said.

I remembered the villages I had visited. They stood gallantly over hilltops. The streams, sparkling with a thousand stars, flowed in the valley's depths. People went downhill to collect water, balancing themselves easily as they slid down the valley. There were no old, bent people. There were only people with smiling, wrinkled faces and lean and energetic bodies like the mountain deer. Nature was benevolent. In a turn of the gravel-laden path here and there, fresh water jutted out from the depths of Mother Earth. Long hollow bamboo poles were sometimes stuck to the mouth of these springs so water could flow through them some distance to the houses nearby. Many of the houses had their natural perennial springs. I thought of them as the wealthiest people on the earth.

Only a little grew on this hilly red earth. It could only be tamed to grow cabbage and cauliflower, capsicum and beans in pockets where there was some even land. But bananas and mangoes, sweet oranges and jackfruits, pumpkins and grapefruits grew independently. Ginger and turmeric could grow on the slopes.

They grew rice near the gurgling streams. It was their staple diet. Most of them had two meals a day of rice and boiled vegetables with fish, pork, or chicken. Most of their food was homegrown. They drank from the spring waters and breathed in the morning air. I loved their red cheeks and the air of happiness that surrounded them. I never saw a long face in all my ears there.

You are connected to your source when you live on and off the land. Are not our bodies an offspring of this mother earth? From her, we gather our bodies, and to her, we return every ounce of them.

We are guests on this earth. But once here, we forget this truth and spend our lives trying to own parts of it until the moment of reckoning comes on the death bed. Then, we wonder at the futility of all things material. How much is enough for one to live comfortably?

I came back to the present when Elisha spoke.

"We feel lonely without our children and the grandchildren."

"But you do have each other, isn't it?" I asked.

"Oh, that we do, and our mother and aunties live with us. We have a wonderful company," they said and departed.

I smiled at their receding backs and wondered. Any other relationship can never override the bonds we share with our siblings. Our cores lay bare in front of them. We can happily continue to be ourselves in their presence. No offence and defence are required. It's a privilege to be close to them in the evening twilight of our lives. These are the times when minimal but wholesome sustenance is required, which comes naturally from loving siblings.

CHAPTER 5

THE DOG'S GRACE

The three of us stood cuddled together as the platform trembled in anticipation. The train roared in, speeding past our collective spinning heads. We breathed a sigh of relief when it stopped. But it was short-lived. Mayhem had ensued, with people rushing in towards their bogies and others trying to fall out of their bogies at the same time. I could not hide a smile. I found elders less intelligent than kids at times.

A long whistle broke my trance. We all then scrambled up to the compartment, following my father. My mother did the same after us.
The train had already started snaking its way. Swaying in tandem with the train, we finally found our seats and sat on them with a thud.
At five years old, I was the eldest of three siblings. The other two were three and two years of age.

All the passengers slipped into a deep slumber while I watched the serene forest rush away silently. My mother groaned. She had a bad toothache. Looking at her, I knew the pain was excruciating. The medicines were of little help.
Besides, she skipped taking the medicines the doctor had advised. Almost all of them affected her adversely. Instead of removing the toothache, they added stomach ache to her repertoire of illnesses. Since I could do but little about it, I watched her helplessly.
   She attempted to smile when she saw my concerned face. My mother was the sunshine herself. The day she could not dazzle, everything seemed dark. Despite the pain, she got up at 3 a.m., lit the coal chullah, and packed parathas with curries for

us. We kids had just managed to get ourselves ready for this trip. A long journey awaited us.

It would be longer for my mother. After scrambling through the multiple bags, we concluded that the medicines had been laid to rest at home. Other, more important things to her were accompanying us. After a couple of hours, the continuing forests stopped enchanting. We had food and laid ourselves to sleep. My mother could eat nothing.

My father woke us up in the middle of the night. "We need to get down. Our intermediate station has arrived," he told us.

The station was lit up in places. We waited as my father went to a counter to book a room for us in the station itself. Soon after, my father returned triumphantly with a key. We all tried to sleep while my mother remained seated on a chair, holding her face in her hands. One side of it had become swollen.

The sky paled. Birds started chirping. A cool breeze was blowing.

"I shall go and throw the remaining food in the dustbin. It is of no use anyway," she said.
I followed her. A dog sat a little away from the room, near the platform's far end.
"The dog seems hungry. I will give this to him," Mother said as she unpacked the food and placed it near him.
We sat on a nearby bench. The dog ate hungrily as we watched from a distance. I was mortally scared of dogs, and it was only because of my mother's presence that I did not make myself scarce.

After relishing the food to the last morsel, the dog looked up. Its shy eyes were filled with gratitude and warmth. He looked at my mother for some time and walked away.

We came back, and our hearts were light. Have you noticed how good one feels when he genuinely serves another being?
Those eyes touched a part of me that day. I felt as if we all were one...

The next train was only an hour away. We went about getting ready when I heard her humming. I looked up in surprise. Her face wore a surprise in return. She tapped on her cheek. She touched her tooth.
"My pain has disappeared!" She blurted out.
My father sprang to his feet. His face was awash with relief.
"I will get some food for you," he said, leaving hurriedly.

Four decades hence, I still remember those shy, lustrous eyes filled with gratitude.

CHAPTER 6

LIFE GOES ON

My final M.B.B.S. exams were fast approaching. I studied every moment I could, and so did my friends in the hostel. The lavatory door had symptoms of particular diseases written on papers stuck to it. I could understand the Lavatory door stickers, but the ones on the bathroom door baffled me no end. They put the stickers in transparent plastic to safeguard them from having a bath themselves!

I was waiting with bated breath for the results, though the exams were still three months away. The result would fulfil my childhood dream of becoming a Doctor. Students went for extra classes covertly, arranged by their proximity to senior students. One's loss was another's gain. I felt tired of it because no special contacts could provide me with a similar edge. That left me mainly to my own devices.

I found solace in my mother's weekend visits. Holding her hand tightly as she slept, I poured over the books until the wee hours of the morning. Soon, the exams started. There was no breather in between the examination days. One after the other, they rolled on. I thought I did well. One early morning, there was a loud knock on the door. Jumping up in fright, I opened the door hurriedly to my mother.
"You are still sleeping! It is past 6 a.m. Today, you have your surgery examination, isn't it?" She said, agitated.
"I slept at four a.m. after completing my studies," I said, trying to calm her down.
"Have a bath soon. I will do 'Puja' now. You come and seek blessings after that," she said.

Feeling disturbed, I rushed with my bucket towards the bathroom at the far end. My mother was a calm

and quiet person. What could make her suddenly agitated? I could think of no explanation for her behaviour. The bath did not feel relaxing that day.
"Mamma, all is well at home, isn't it?" I asked softly.
"Yes, of course. What can go wrong at home? I do all that is required and then come here to wish you luck," she said.

It was too much of a strain on her. She had to leave all my younger siblings and come early to see me. My brother was only five years old then. She had to get up at three A.M. to make it here. I suddenly felt very guilty.

"It is all right. I will manage the rest of the examination myself. Please do not trouble yourself anymore." I told her.
"I come because I want to see my child before she leaves for a crucial exam. You might be older than my other children, but you are still a child for me," she said as she packed my pen and other things.
As I hurriedly got ready, I suddenly remembered.
"Please read out this chapter of Cholecystitis," I pointed out the pages to her.
I gulped my breakfast and ran out of the hostel as she read.
"Do well," she cried as I did so.

I strode as I reached near the exam centre. I was feeling very distressed. It felt as if my core had survived an earthquake and was grappling with its aftereffects.

My exam went well. Since it was Friday, I would have two days to prepare for the next exam. As I walked back, I thought of an old friend of mine. I had not spoken to her for the last ten years, but she had constantly been popping into my mind's eye from the preceding week. I would meet her once I went back home after the exams.

My mother was anxiously waiting for me in the hostel. She knew from my face that I had done well, and she smiled in satisfaction. We had lunch, and then she started to leave.

At the door, she stopped for a moment and said hesitantly, "I wanted to tell you about Tarannum, but I don't know whether I should or not."
My heart missed a beat.
"Tarannum! I can't stop thinking about her. Did something happen to her?" I cried, agitated.
"She is not well," she said.
"Is that all? She is just not well?" I cried, my heart beating fast.
She stood at the door quietly.

"She has got ninety per cent burns. They admitted her to the burn ward of our hospital. I was there all night with her yesterday," she said slowly, her eyes lined with tears.

I felt myself sinking. She returned and put her hands on my head, and then, since she would miss the bus if she stayed any longer, she went away.

Tarannum was my childhood friend. We were together from our Kindergarten days. Her house was on the way to our school. So I invariably called out to her, and then we walked together for the rest of the way. She was a fair and a bright girl. We both shared the same weakness. Our bodies were full of funny bones. Little things made us explode with laughter at a moment's notice, to the great annoyance of our teachers. They ensured that we sat in two opposite corners of the room so that the wave of laughter of our making did not engulf everyone else in the class.

Strangely, I did not laugh much when alone. Once I finished seventh grade, I went off to study in a school in another city, and she continued in the same place in a different school. I left early in the morning at 5:30 a.m. and returned at 7:30 p.m. There was no time to meet her, so we drifted apart.

Once, I saw her on a Sunday, surrounded by her friends, mostly boys, but she was busy talking and did not notice me.

Years flew by. I got admitted to medical school and started staying in a hostel. At the same time, she fell in love.

Love turned her life upside down. She belonged to a family of orthodox Muslims. The person she loved was from a different community. The family was devout to the extent that the news of his son falling in love with a Muslim girl gave the father a heart attack. He barely survived after recuperating in the hospital for more than a month.

Her own family did not approve of it, either. They put her under house arrest, and a frantic search started for a Muslim bridegroom. They found a 'perfect' match for her. He was a widower twenty-five years her senior and had four kids. At such short notice, they could arrange only this. This was her destiny, they declared.

Tarannum wept, locked in her room with little mercy shown by her parents. Her boyfriend, Salem, was transferred to a distant place at the behest of his influential father. He was a Senior Engineer in the same organisation.

Tarannum marriage day was fast approaching, and hushed preparations were going on. It was to be solemnized in a faraway place. Her little sister, Suhana, was appalled at all this. She smuggled food into her room whenever she could and tried to convince her neighbours to help her sister. Their heart went out for the joyous girl Tarannum. It was a closely knit society, and they tried to make her father see reason, but to no avail.

The ripples created in the locality spread near and far. On the day of their departure, Tarannum, on the pretext of something, ran away... ran away from it all to freedom.

Some people helped her, and she ultimately reached Salem's dwelling, where they married secretly and registered their marriage in court.

The news spread like wildfire, and the families immediately disowned their children. Tarannum's family went one step further and performed the funeral rites of their daughter!

I did get a glimpse of her when I went home for a few days two years back. She looked happy and glowing as she walked with her husband, leaning on his arm. By the time I could run and call her, they had moved a great distance. I would meet her some other day, I had thought then. It was said that her husband's family had finally accepted them. Love for the son had dissolved the hatred. Love is all-encompassing.

Her happy face had calmed my being. I joined my final year, and then her memories faded away.

Ninety per cent burns meant she would be in terrible pain. I had seen such patients in the hospital. I found it difficult to stand before them. My hands trembled, and tears blinded me at the intense agony I witnessed. They could neither sit nor stand. Some could not lie down—human bodies without skin...burned faces. Many times, I would break down while trying to dress their wounds. I remember a nurse who had driven me away from the burn ward seeing me like that.

"Come back only when you are fit to be a doctor," she had said.

'God give no one so much pain.'
I prayed within me, and now my dear friend was facing the same. My grief knew no words. I could hardly understand what I was reading. I could have met her but did not have the courage. I could not see her in that state.

My mother came on Monday morning.
"She is recovering," she said a little too brightly as she answered my unasked question.

Deep down in my heart, I knew she was nearing her end. My exam somehow went all right, and God's grace was there for me despite having hardly studied anything.
"How did she get burnt, Mamma?" I asked.
My mother hesitated as if debating whether to answer.
"Tell me," I persisted.
"The kerosene stove burst while she was cooking," she whispered.
"Nobody uses kerosene any more for cooking. All households have LPG connections now. Why was she still using it?" I asked, surprised.
"How is she there? I thought she was with her husband," I persisted with my questions.

My mother looked down, knowing not what to answer. Her silence increased my anxiety.
"She was nine months pregnant. She had come for her delivery at her in-law's house. Her husband left

her in his parent's care and returned to his workplace," she said.
Silence...

My mother left after some time. She could not come to see me for the next couple of days. Medicine was my last exam subject.

The night before the exam, I studied hard. It was a vast subject; a substantial part remained, even past two a.m. Sitting on the chair, cramped in one position for so long, I felt tired. I moved about in the corridor in front of my room. Sleep seemed to cloud my eyes. I washed my face and went to the Television room. It was a large hall with long benches arranged in rows and a television in a corner. It was our entertainment corner on Sundays. Now, it was all empty.

I closed the door from inside and arranged two benches with backrests in front of each other. I then sat on one and spread out my feet on another, keeping the book on my lap. Thus seated comfortably, I skimmed over the remaining chapters. It was about four a.m. My eyes felt heavy and seemed to close on their own.

Suddenly, I woke up with a start and heard someone calling my name. It was Tarannum, seated on the opposite bench, next to my feet! I watched her, amazed. She looked beautiful in a light pink gown.

"See, I am not burnt at all," she said, lifting her gown to her knees and spreading her arms and hands in front of me.
I gazed at her fair skin and face and exclaimed in astonishment, "Really! Imagine my mother fooling

me like that! I thought you were burnt. I could not stop grieving."
"No, I am perfectly fine," she said and threw her head back, laughing loudly.
I broke into a loud laughter and threw my head back, too. We were laughing together after a decade.

Strange are our eyes' ways. When we are laughing our hearts out, they close on their own.
When I opened my eyes, Tarannum had vanished! I was laughing all alone.

Where did she go? I called out to her.
"Come on, do not hide from me. We are not kids any more. Where are you hiding?"
That's so typical of her! I removed the big fat book from my lap, got down from the bench, and started looking for her below the benches. I kept calling her as I did so. How could she disappear?

Both doors were still latched from inside. Suddenly, a strange, intense fear gripped me. I grabbed the book. I wanted to rush back into my own room. The door latch seemed too tight. My hands were trembling. I opened the door with great difficulty and dashed into my room. I locked the door tight and, with shaking hands, closed the windows. I put off the light and covered myself totally with the quilt. My heart was jumping inside me.
'Oh God, save me... save me...' I said to myself.
I know not when I drifted away to sleep. I awoke when there was a loud knock on my door. It was six-thirty a.m. My mother had come.
"You are still sleeping! Have you finished studying?" She asked.
I nodded.

"Tarannum...," she started saying.
I interrupted her.
"She is no more, isn't it so?" I asked.
She nodded, looking surprised and said, "She died at 4 A.M. today."

"She had to bear so much pain. Her parents, though near, did not visit her even once. She kept asking for them. We requested them, but their hearts..."
Silence.
"We did her funeral preparations. The gown stuck to her in a way that we could not remove it," she said, turning away to wipe a tear.
"That light pink gown... isn't it?" I blurted out.
"How do you know this?"
"She had come to meet me at 4 a.m. Mamma. There is not a single burn injury on her body now. She is free of pain and happy. We both could not stop laughing like in the good old days," I told her.

She watched me speechless. Then she broke into a smile.

Tarannum's 'visitation' had calmed us both. There was no more pain.

CHAPTER 7

THE LITTLE GHOST

My family stayed in a small Colony. Rows and rows of residential quarters stood proudly on either side of black, shining tarred roads. There were many vacant large tracks of land interspersed between them. Cows and goats lazily grazed all day there till the Sun dipped down in the far horizon. I always attended these final moments of rendezvous with the setting sun. The sky turned yellow, deep orange, pink, greyish blue, and dark. The fresh new painting of the Creator every day left me enthralled. I loved to be alone at such times. It was that time of the day when I seemed to become one with the earth, sky and the sun. The exquisite feeling of absolute stillness and peace has stayed with me ever since.

As the darkness crept in, I became aware of the Mango tree against that backdrop, which stood about ten metres away from me. It had seemed perfectly harmless until then. Suddenly, it seemed to come up alive. The hundreds of birds on it would fall silent, and a hundred eyes seemed to open and stare at me from there. I would know then that it was time for me to go back home.

On my way back, the gory tales I had heard of Ghosts hanging out on that tree would flood my brain. Did ghosts really exist? I would find out once I grew up. The only information that I had gathered by eavesdropping on softly whispered tales of elders was that they loved white, for they always donned that colour, besides, of course, swaying.

Each house had a big courtyard shaped like a capital 'C'. Probably, each house was caught in the claws of a crab, which would describe them better. Many of them had gardens and giant trees of Guava and Mango. We also had them in our garden. I loved the Guava tree. It was my friend, for I remained hidden in one of its branches, reading books, singing happy songs and sharing my day's adventures. The tree patiently heard them, nodded, and smiled, rustling its leaves or swaying its branches.

The Mango tree disappointed me hugely.
It grew straight, towering up towards the sky without lending me a branch to climb on. I understood that it held children with a quiet disregard. To top it all, its fruits were a total disgrace!
What kind of tree gave forth fruits whose seeds were as big as the fruit? Monkeys on that tree would throw those stony mangoes at us, striking us in return for the stones we pelted on them for teasing us.

My friends would make fun of our mangoes, infuriating me further.
"You do not even know how to make a mango, you silly tree! Have you never heard of anything called 'pulp'? Do you think a mango has only a seed and a skin? Next year, do better than this. Do you understand? " I would tell it loudly.

The best Mango tree in our locality grew in the last house of our row. They were huge and sweet. The owner loved our children's troop and allowed us to raid the tree. But there was a problem: his watchman Kumar. Short and dark, he refused to let us have even one mango from that tree. Our group of children, of which I was the leader, waited in the late afternoons for him to fall asleep. Those were the days when all elders took a small nap during that time.

That day, I had just climbed the tree after climbing up the boundary wall while the others waited on the other side. As I vigorously shook the mango-laden branch, the 'thap thap' sound of falling mangoes awakened him. He came rushing towards me with a stick twice my size. In absolute panic, I jumped off the tree to the other side and escaped as fast as possible. Back home, I was sure the mangoes would be weeping in his tummy.

Though only six years old, I had quite the mean streak in me and would not take this lying down. Soon, the opportunity presented itself.

My father would wake us up at 4 a.m. every day and take us for a walk with neem toothbrushes in our mouths. By the time we came back, the sky would start turning blue. At such an early twilight moment one day, I saw Kumar walking a little distance in the street opposite my house. A bright idea struck me instantly at his sight.

I rushed in and wrapped myself in a plain white bed sheet. As he approached, I started swaying slowly, as if dancing to a slow, distant English tune. The effect was dramatic.

He stared in horror, and his large eyes grew bigger and bigger.
"Ore Baba! Ore Baba! (Oh, father!) Chotto booth (small ghost) ...!" he said, gasping, as his hands covered his mouth.
Then he lifted his lungee to the knees and ran away as fast as he could, yelling, " Bhoot! Bhoot!"

I dropped to the floor, helpless with laughter. The laughing cost me dear, for in the process, I got so

51

entangled in the vast bed sheet that extricating myself from the mess was quite an ordeal. It was my good fortune that no one saw me in such a state, for I would have a lot of explanation to give.

That evening, a solemn-looking Kumar came to warn my mother of a 'little booth' in our house. My mother refused to listen to him, and I realised she had little regard for him.

The owner's wife followed him on his visit. To make my mother understand, she exaggerated the description, matching it with eyes that became rounder and bigger with time.
The little ghost flew about the house. It had a sinister face and was bent on harming. Other ghosts were beside it, flying and flapping their wings!
Sitting with my book right there, I tried my best not to burst into laughter. Hiding my face behind my book, I hoped my mother would not smell a rat. She did not. I survived that day.

Kumar turned over a new leaf and respectfully handed me the number of mangoes I demanded the next time. He no longer ran after kids with a stick or threw stones at them. Instead, he treated them with respect.

I would have become a devotee of that ghost if it had not been me.

I do not know why he never looked directly at me. Did my size bother him? Did he see an uncanny resemblance in my eyes? I will never know this, but the memory of that escapade still makes me smile, even after so many years.

CHAPTER 8

MY ENGLISH TEACHER

The bus stopped after some hesitant jerks. We gave a collective moan. This sudden snag meant another wait in the school bus for how long we did not know. Our bus took us to and fro from our colony every day. The sixty students in it were an eclectic mix of students from different schools and colleges. All had other times of closing. So even though we finished ours by 1. p.m., we could start to return home only at 6.30 p.m. This was when the last college student would jump onto the bus.

How our hearts rejoiced then silently. Silently because our strict driver did not like loud rejoicings, all of us together could dish out quite a racket, so much so that he would lose whatever patience he had and would park the bus in a deep jungle on the way back, put off the lights and to our utter dismay, leave us in complete darkness and walk off! So, stuck in that God-forbidden jungle, where we could feel but not see the face of the person sitting next, we learnt DISCIPLINE.

But that day, we had been perfectly civil, and because of a quirk of fate, the bus had stopped on its own somewhere near a college. My stomach was growling. It was about 5 p.m. Unfortunately, the lunch box packed by my mother had been too difficult to resist, and I had finished the last morsel by 7 a.m. We started from home before dawn and would be ravenously hungry by the time we reached school at 6.30 a.m.

At that opportune time, a familiar voice called me by my name. Mrs Iris Wilkinson, my favourite teacher who taught us English, was calling me.

"What are you doing here?" Her straightforward, lyrical voice asked me.
I told her about our dilemma.
"You reach home at 7.30 p.m. every day!" She gasped with a look of consternation on her fair face.
"Come in," she added.

I got down and walked up to her. It felt so lovely seeing her.
"This is my house. Come in," she said.
I felt shy and a little hesitant. I had the former in abundance, though I need help pinpointing its reason. It was a natural trait, an unwelcome one at that. It never really helped me. Why! I was even shy of looking into the eyes of anyone who ever spoke to me. I preferred the uninteresting ground instead.
"Come in. Bring all your friends too," she said.
"But we are almost sixty of us, Miss."
"It is all right. Come in."
I ran up to the other students.
"My Miss is calling all of us. Come down, all of you, and follow me," I told them grandly.
I took our driver's permission before telling the others. I had no wish to lock horns with the Tiger himself. I know not why he looked relieved.

It was a large bungalow with a beautiful garden. We all spread into the unfamiliar rooms like a kaleidoscope. It felt so good compared to the stuffy school bus. They brought the cups and glasses out, and we had coffee, cookies, sweetmeats and cakes. Those were not the days of paper and plastic cups. So, all came in different sizes and designs. The transparent glass cups and the ceramic ones shone. Miss used to store cakes and sweetmeats in tins! As we concentrated on the delicacies, I saw Miss looking at all of us with a smile and contentment. A

55

swift two hours passed away, and we left reluctantly only after we heard the shrill horn of the bus at length!

My friends and senior college students gave me furtive glances on the way home. Some faces that did not know how to wear a smile did that day. I felt grateful and proud of her.

Over three decades later, I still feel overwhelmed by that gesture of hers. This is especially true when I must entertain sudden guests and feel inundated and exasperated with the sudden elaborate preparation required.
I could imbibe some knowledge from her magnificent presence but not her kindness and greatness of heart. Some things cannot be taught. They blossom forth from the deepest recesses of the heart like those rare flowers of the mighty Himalayas.

CHAPTER 9

UNSEEN WORLD

She had been reluctantly pulled into a circle. The circle consisted of closed-knit family members sitting on the floor and staring intently at the middle. An old lady sat on one side, her face covered with the end of her saree. She seemed old and frail. All eyes alternated between her face and the ground in the middle of the circle.

Tanu felt very uncomfortable. She wanted to leave the place.
She was about to stand up when her mother-in-law looked at her with eyes full of disapproval.

"Once in here, no one can leave," the old lady said softly.
She then turned her veiled face towards the mother-in-law.
"Who is she?" She asked.
"My daughter-in-law, the bride of my second son, does not believe in these things. What do you make of her?" she asked.
There was a sudden silence. The clock ticked away.
   The veiled lady turned slowly towards Tanu. Tanu baulked as the lady studied her minutely, her face still hidden. There was a veil, but it was not a veil, for she could see clearly despite it.
Moments of tense silence ensued. The lady then broke into a smile...
"She is just afraid of this. She is good," she said suddenly with a fondness.
The tension gave away a bit.

"Close your eyes. I am calling him," the veiled lady said with a sudden finality.
All did so at once.

Tanu watched everyone intently. The fear was now replaced with curiosity. They had said that something would surface in the middle of the circle. She observed from her slit eyes. This had to be fake.

The circle was big. She watched the hands of everyone. They were all open, with the palms stretched out. All the windows and doors were closed. She checked out the ventilators. They were securely locked. The room light was dim. The faint light of the setting sun shone on the ventilator glass.

She concentrated again in the middle.
"Give me eight talismans. They need your protection," the lady ordered.
Then, her voice changed into that of another.
"Uff, this is too difficult. It is painful for me. Manage with four. Please manage with four of them," the voice was groaning as if in pain.
"I want eight of them, one for each of my family members," my mother-in-law insisted.

"I am trying. Give me...give me...uff...uff...give me. I told you to give...," the lady commanded and then moaned.

Tanu was excited by then. She stared at the lady. She would probably quietly put some in the middle.
"They are coming. Yes, they are coming!" The lady said joyfully.

Tanu looked at the ventilator glass. It would probably shatter, and they would fall in, she thought. She again shot a quick look at the lady's hidden hands and then that of the others. They all sat with eyes closed in anticipation, their palms stretched out. She looked at the ground in the middle, and then

59

her heart almost stopped beating! A handful of Talismans appeared in there from nowhere! She looked behind her. THERE WAS NO ONE.

There was a sudden jubilation all around. The lady seemed exhausted. Her mother-in-law held all of them as if they were a handful of diamonds. Tanu remained fascinated and excited, suspicious and fearful.
What was all this?

She had spent all her previous life in a city. Her scientific mind dissected the scene minutely, repeatedly. Had she missed something?

Perhaps a very important clue. But then they suddenly sprang up right in front of her studying eyes. She wanted to leave. Her mother-in-law had more questions. Someone had harmed them by casting a dark spell.
 Tanu sprang up with a shot. She could not bear it anymore. She opened the door and ran out. The others kept yelling, asking her to stop. She did not look back and rushed up the stairs to her infant daughter.

"What's wrong? You look upset," the maid said, alarmed when she saw her.
 "There is nothing wrong with me. Do make a strong cup of tea for me with ginger," she told her.
She wanted to be alone. Her child smiled warmly, cycling her little feet rapidly in the air. Caressing her in her arms, she soon forgot the strange occurring below.

It was after two hours that her mother-in-law came into the Shiva temple on their floor. The time of evening prayers had long passed. She was excited and brimming with information.

"You ran away from there. What did not emerge from below the foundation of our building?" she said excitedly on seeing her.

Tanu stared in disbelief.
"How did they dig below this building?" She asked.
"So silly you are! She just asked the spirits, and they emerged with my personal items in that circle: a part of my saree, which I used to wear thirty years ago, strands of my hair, and so many other things," she added.
"What does it mean?" Tanu looked askance at her.
"It simply means that wicked people, our enemies, have been trying to hurt us for a long time. They stole these personal items of mine to cast a dark spell. I have had trying times all through my life! Today, I have uprooted it completely. Of course, I have paid quite a hefty sum to bring that lady here," she said triumphantly.

Tanu did not know what to think. It still seemed fake, but she had seen it with her own eyes.
Was it real, or was she hallucinating?

"You wear this talisman and tie this one around your daughter's right arm."
Mother-in-law's voice brought her back to the present.
"I don't need this," Tanu protested.
"You will have to do as I say," she said sternly.
Tanu remained adamant.

"This is for your good. This is to keep your daughter safe. You know not what great harm will come on her otherwise. You have no idea about all this," she added.

Her husband joined the rhetoric, too. Sometimes, Tanu wondered whether he had his senses intact. She slid the talisman around her arm and that of her child. It seemed like a weird thing sticking on to her.

Oh God, keep us all safe! What awful things went on in this strange, forested land? She thought of her own city. A sudden sigh escaped her.

A week passed off awkwardly. She felt as if she was being watched constantly... by whom she could not tell. She asked the others. All were wearing them and were at ease. The nagging feeling continued in her. She brushed it aside as a figment of her imagination.

It was early evening. The orange sun had left mild traces of its colour on the far horizon and had slipped into slumber. The rest of the sky was bluish-grey and dark. The temple bells were ringing. Conch shells were being blown in the neighbourhood houses. Tanu, watching all this from the terrace, rushed downstairs to her floor. It was time for evening puja. The rooms were still dark. Her daughter was sleeping peacefully. Light filtered from the corridor tube light. She bent over to wake up her daughter.

It was then when someone bent over her... Strong arms encircled her from behind, towering over her and gripping her tightly.
Terror-stricken, she tried to shout but could not. Her feet were frozen.
"Oh Shiva...Oh, Shiva...please help...." she repeatedly said within her.

He suddenly let her go, and his grip loosened. She clasped her child in her arms and rushed outside into the lighted corridor. She jerked the talismans out of their arms and flung them onto the floor.

Her daughter clung to her in panic as Tanu watched the two talismans dancing with great energy on the floor in utter disbelief.
When they stopped, her heart was still beating wildly.
"Oh, Shiva..."

When she emerged from the adjoining Shiva temple, her mother-in-law stared furiously at her as she stood near the fallen talismans.
"You cannot even..." she started saying.
Tanu interrupted her.

"Why have you built a Shiva temple in your house when you have no faith in him? If you have faith, then why do you call in the dark forces to watch over us?" Tanu interjected.

Both fell silent at this sudden recognition.
PROTECTION BY DARK UNSEEN FORCES!

Tanu threw the two talismans into a distant pool of water, and the splash seemed to calm her down.
She had learnt a hard lesson. She would need it to survive in this strange land.

CHAPTER 10

CRIES OF REGRET

The big desk curved around us as we sat relaxed. It was cold. The fog settled over the valleys and the pine tops in a misty white. I liked to think it had gone and settled in my lungs. I loved the freshness it imparted to me as I went to work in the morning.

The heaters burned a golden yellow near my feet. Its jaws were widely open in anticipation.
"Be careful," the nurse, sitting beside me, rolled her eyes knowingly.
I flushed. I burned the soles of my shoes the last time I was there, resting them absent-mindedly, directly on them.
Only when we could not find the source of the burning smell, even after checking everything about the large casualty room, did someone notice it.
As a result, he yelled so loudly that I almost jumped out of my skin and screamed louder than him. In the sudden tumult, my feet got so entangled in the mass of wires that my shoes were thrown off, and everyone gaped.
HOW COULD YOU?

The soles of my shoes had become syrupy and laid themselves out flat with twisted horns at the end.

I have this quirk of getting so absorbed in reading that I become oblivious to the world around me.
I blamed it on the lack of patients that morning. If they had been around, I would not have had the opportunity to chill on that chair with my feet perched up like that. No one agreed to that, and they merely laughed at my predicament and my syrupy shoes.

Dr. Ben came in just then and sat himself with a thud on the chair next to me.
"Where were you?"
It sounded more like, "Where were you while I burned?"
He was on duty along with me and had surfaced just then. He immediately explained about the sudden boil that had surfaced on his geography some time back, and he had to get the nurse to incise and drain it.

"He gets it all the time," the other nurse waved her hand dismissively.
"You get this all the time!" I blurted out.
"No doctor, not all the time. She loves to exaggerate," he said sheepishly.
"But why is your immunity status so pathetic?"
He shrugged his shoulders and looked down.

Both nurses winked at me, and I looked askance at them. I can never understand this winking in general. It is done impromptu at different times to convey messages that are always worlds apart.

One whispered in my ears when he moved away to the other end of the room.
"He is a drug addict, Madam, and please try your best not to look surprised."
I didn't. I inadvertently looked disgusted instead.

How could physicians turn themselves into drug addicts? What was the use of years of study? How would he help his patients if he did not know how to help himself?
She read my thoughts.
"He has a young wife and a six-month-old child," she said.

I wished to give him a long discourse but decided against it. You can never help someone if he has no wish to support himself.

It was about 8 a.m. that day. The children had left for school. I had made a tall, frothy cup of coffee for myself and was about to sip when loud voices broke inside my head.
I HAVE WRONGED MY WIFE. I HAVE WRONGED MY KIDS.

I dropped my cup on the table and rushed outside to the balcony. Who was saying that? A few people strolled on the road, but none were talking. It was in my head.

The voice started getting louder and more urgent. I pressed my hands to my ears, but the voice would not stop.

I was not a stranger to these voices in my head. When I started hearing them many years ago, I thought I was going mad. I had thought that I needed psychiatric treatment. Not any more...

After years of trying to unravel the strange visions and whispers, after years of seeking answers and finding them, and after years of esoteric studies, I knew or could correctly guess the answers.

Someone had done something wrong and was regretting it. But who was it? More importantly, why did I hear his lament?

For three days, I could neither eat nor sleep. The voice continued, repeating those lines with so much

emotion and intensity that I found it hard to keep myself sane.
STOP! STOP! Why are you shouting? Why are you telling me? Who are you? What can I do?

He did not stop. I realised he could not stop because he was not talking to me. Unfortunately, my ears could somehow pick up his words.
By the end of ten days, the lack of sleep and the constant drumming made me so weak that I could hardly take myself to work.

'Please help me, God. I cannot take this anymore. Please help.'

Slowly, the voice became faint, and I could hear it only if I concentrated enough. The urgency in the voice had disappeared, and a sad resignation had seeped in. Then, it disappeared altogether.

I was failing in something. There must have been a reason for my hearing that voice. Who was he? What did he want from me? But it never addressed me. I had just overheard it. Why?

"So, you have not heard about it!" My colleague said, looking at me intently as she sipped her tea.
"What do I not know? You know I am in my big cocoon and love to stay inside it," I replied.
"Dr. Ben died of an inadvertent overdose two weeks back."

I jumped straight out of my chair. The teacup I was holding emptied itself on me.
"I did not know that he was your close acquaintance!" She said.

I gathered myself together and nodded in the negative.

My mind was racing. It was him. I had not recognised his voice. How could I? I had met him a couple of times while doing duty together and had spoken to him only on a few occasions. I did not know that he had left his body.

She was watching me intently.
"You want to go and console his wife. She does not need your services."
"Do you know her?'
"Not really. She is a physician like him and has a daughter who is a few months old."

My heart went out to her.
"We have to face whatever situation arises in our lives stoically," she said.
I nodded.

I dare not tell her. If I did, she would think that I had lost my mind and perhaps take me to our psychiatrist colleague immediately.

I must meet the wife and convey what I had overheard. But how could I? No one whom I knew had her contact details. What would I tell her if I did get her phone number? Would she believe me?

The nagging pain in my heart continued. I was failing Dr. Ben in some way...

Then Covid happened. It turned our lives upside down. I spent so much time in the hospital that it became my home. I almost lost touch with my home and kids. They survived on stale bread and water.

The whole hospital had to be revamped, and extended duty hours had to be imposed ....

"I strongly object to this. She should not be given these 24-hour duties. Please understand. She has an infant who has no father. What if she gets affected and succumbs to it?" I said in the committee meeting.

"How is that a matter of your concern?"

I suddenly felt responsible for the safety of his family.
"Hundreds of patients are dying in and around this hospital and all over the town. We cannot think of ourselves during such times," one of the members said.
"The doctors' problems are not our problems. They can leave if they cannot perform their duties," someone said.
"Who will do these taxing duties then? Have you thought about it?" One of the members said.
The meeting was over.

One of the members followed me, "If we think about the personal problems of each doctor here, we will need to shut the hospital doors."
I nodded.
"By the way, how does the duty of one particular doctor concern you?"
He asked.
"Since she is the lone parent...," my voice trailed.
"Do not worry so much. Whatever must happen will happen, and we won't be able to do anything about it."

I had seen her that day. Young and fair, her face was solemn and calm as she sat writing on her desk. She had been appointed to her late husband's post. I could not remove my eyes from her. Perhaps it was a mix of sympathy and empathy, love and affection, and a secret knowing. I felt a strange responsibility towards her. I was invested in her happiness and well-being. I also had a secret to share when she was alone.

I tried to meet her, but patients always surrounded her. I also developed cold feet. This was personal and perhaps outrageous, too. Would she be ready to listen to me? Would she believe me if she did?

One of the members informed us the next time we met, "She is happy doing the extended hours duties."

My heart skipped a beat. I spoke to a few colleagues and discovered that she had left her baby in her mother's care.

I also understood her thought that I had overheard, "Why are you interfering in my life?"
She was right.

I could not bring myself to go up to her and speak about it. Days passed into months, and the burden of the confession weighed heavily on my heart. I had her phone number saved.

The present-day generation has the blessings of the digital world. What cannot be said directly can be put into words and messaged, and a prompt reply can be expected.

"I wished to speak about your late husband. I have a message to share with you."

She did not answer.

"Please believe what I write here. Your husband is very sorry for what he has done. He is filled with guilt and remorse. I understand that you are miffed with him. Please forgive him."
Silence...
"What was your relationship with my husband?"
"I did a few emergency duties with him. I hardly know him. I overheard him saying repeatedly a few lines after his death. I HAVE WRONGED MY WIFE. I HAVE WRONGED MY KIDS. He kept on saying this again and again. He is full of remorse. Please forgive him."
There was no reply for a long time.

I prayed that she would respond. I prayed that she would find the strength. It is not easy to forgive. He had left her all alone with an infant. How could he have been so irresponsible? Did he not care for his child?

"I have only one child."

"He was talking about kids. That is more than one. Is there any other kid that he loved dearly?"

"I have only one child. I do not know about any other."

Was I dreaming? Did I not hear him properly? For about thirteen days, his voice had been constantly drumming into my ears day and night. He had been talking about kids all the time.

Who were the other kids he was talking about?

It was about six months later that I received her message.
"My husband was very close to his sister's son. He used to get him ready for school and drop him. He loved him very much."

"He loved you as well as the kids. He did not realise that he would die so suddenly. His regret is so deep that he cannot be at peace. Please forgive him."

My heart felt heavy. I thought she was weeping; strangely, tears flowed from my eyes.

May we live each day,
In a way, that is right,
The conscience is God's voice,
Showing us the light.

CHAPTER 11

MY MISER UNCLE

The Sun baked them crisp as they stood waiting in long lines. A mere ten years old, he watched anxiously while awaiting his turn. A handful of cooked rice and vegetables was given to each. He would have to share this with his brother back in the tent at the refugee camp. There were six of them, including his mother. His turn to eat once a day came every two days.

His parched throat craved water.

The lush green rice fields swayed in the morning breeze. The spring flowed gurgling happily along. Large pots of rice boiled on the dancing flames of logs of wood. The women of the house sat talking in delight as their hands cut loads of vegetables in precise equal sizes. He had always wondered at their machine fingers. Someday, he would make real machines. He would study in Calcutta. His heart brimmed with dreams. His father shared them. They were affluent, and the troubled times of the partition of India did not affect them much.

Their large estate, which included hundreds of acres of land, produced a surplus of everything they needed. It was a contented life.

Orange-red flames leapt high in the village, touching the skies. They carried the entreaties and agonies of men and women, kids and their elk being burnt alive, along with the stacks of harvested rice. The rioters set a part of their estate on fire. His father suffered a massive heart attack and succumbed as their estate burnt. In the dead of the night, they left with whatever they could carry for New India. Their boat was attacked multiple times. The Padma River turned red with the blood of slaughtered men. Nature hath no fury like that of mad men with hearts of hatred.

The volunteer gazed at the intense eyes lined with tears.

"One day, you will grow so big that your hands can feed hundreds of children. Take heart, my child!" he said as he filled an earthen bowl-shaped plate full of steaming rice and lentils.

Going back, Adhir made a solemn promise to himself.

People gazed at the strange new boy of their locality with amusement. He was solving mathematics problems on the road with a piece of coal. Vehicles were few and far between in those days. The teachers in his school were astonished at his prowess. He could solve complicated sums of senior classes with ease. His reputation grew as a mathematics wizard. By the time he finished school, he had earned a scholarship to fund his studies.

The entire family was proud the day he earned his Engineering degree. He never looked back after that.

His younger brothers raised families, as did his elder ones. He remained unmarried. They tried to find a suitable bride for him. He refused to see their photographs. Some had crooked lips, some had crooked noses, and others had dark or too fair skin. Exasperated, they left him alone, so he stayed all his life, saving every penny he earned.

"I have never spent a single paisa that I have earned. I only live off the interest I earn on it," he told me proudly one day.

I found him weird. He was a high-ranking official who had been given a car with a chauffeur, which he

never used. Instead, he walked to the bus stop and took overcrowded buses to his office.
We kids were in awe of him and afraid of his temper. We wanted to go sightseeing in Calcutta and could not lurch onto the buses overflowing with humanity. I asked him timidly about his official car.
"Why will I use government money for personal comfort?" He asked.

I had no answer to that. I always needed help understanding his two shirts and two trousers wardrobe. On official tours, he travelled by air nationwide and transformed the country's oil sector. He lost an eye while excavating an oil well in one of the country's remote corners but had no regrets. Even after he retired, he was much sought after for his invaluable experience. Tending to his home and hearth all alone, he lived the life of a hermit. We always wondered at his miserly habits. Others laughed at the poor 'Rich' man.

A year back, he called me suddenly one day.
"My child, I know you are capable and do not need anything, but I still have a small gift for you. Use it to sustain yourself in the time of your need. You can pass it on to the next generation if it is not required now and then to the next. None of the next seven generations of our family tree should ever starve. If you invest it well and use it only in the time of your need, it will last. I have worked all my life to ensure only this. Please accept it," he said softly.
A lump formed so hard in my throat that I could not speak. Tears ran down my cheeks. The line disconnected suddenly then.

No one in the vast family had remained untouched by his benevolence. His donations benefitted

children's homes and orphanages, educational institutions for poor children, and philanthropic organisations.
 My Miser uncle... I am so proud of him.

CHAPTER 12

THE HOODED MAN

The house overlooked a newly made road. On the horizon was a forested area, home to many birds: parrots, pigeons, hornbills, mynas, and many more. "Most of the birds have disappeared," one of the neighbours told me.
"They were such a pleasant sight. They flew down to this balcony and picked from our hands. But they do not fly down here anymore," another lady lamented.
"It is not that we miss them. They cannot be given toilet training like we do for our dogs and cats. Once they leave, the place shines with their droppings. I hate it," a lady said.

I understood their predicament. I blamed the pigeons for it. They pecked as many times as you offered them and pooped as many times. I thought they had perennial diarrhoea.

"There is another reason for the birds to move away from our locality. We all know about it," an old lady chimed in.
They had gathered on the balcony of my rented apartment and talked among themselves. I was busy going in and out of the kitchen, serving them tea and snacks, so I missed much of the ensuing conversation.

"What is the reason?"
 They looked at each other and then fell quiet.
"We do not wish to scare you…"
"I am a brave person. You can tell me," I said.
"Do you see the stream flowing down here?"
I asked, "Do you mean the drain between the buildings on one side and the road on the other?"

A lady bit her tongue on hearing that.

"You should never make fun of nature's bounty and God's grace. This stream is a blessing to all of us. It is a perennial source of water for those who live here. In the summer, when the taps run dry, this stream is our lifeline," one lady said.
"But it is so dirty! Who can drink such water?" I blurted out.
"People do not drop into the flowing stream and take drinking water out. If you notice carefully, springs emerge from the depths of the earth, and their mouths open into this stream. People crowd there from the break of dawn to get fresh water as it falls from a height into this."

I remember people lining up far away. They were like shadows moving in the morning mist.
"I have grown up drinking this water right from childhood," one lady informed.

I failed to see the connection between the spring and the bird's disappearance.

"This happened about ten years ago. In this neighbourhood, a girl and a boy were deeply in love. They studied in a college in this city and planned to marry after graduation. Their parents disapproved because they belonged to different communities. One morning, their bodies floated by our house," one of the ladies who lived on the right side of the apartment building said.

Silence...

"Before you start wondering at the ankle-deep water in this now, which you cannot see until you bend over the balcony rim, let me tell you that the stream was about five to six feet at its breadth and had a depth of more than ten feet. In the mornings, it shone in a way that made us feel as if it were loaded with thousands and thousands of diamonds."

How I wish it had been so still. How lovely it would be to have a stream flow near your balcony, and you could watch it while sipping your morning cuppa.

"There were drastic changes in the stream after that. There can be no logical reason for this, but the water level has ebbed. And then there were the 'visits...,'" one of the ladies said.

The air was pregnant with suspense. A shiver ran down my spine. But no one continued the story further.
"What do you mean by the visits?"
They looked at each other as if a sudden weight rested on their tongues. I could see fear in some of their eyes. They got up and left hurriedly, one after the other.

I could understand the 'visits'. Their spirits probably had not found peace and could not ascend to the realm they were supposed to move into after their death.
   I was not a stranger to ghosts. I felt and, at times, saw them from my childhood days. But every time I encountered them, I was overcome with fear.

I had shifted to this apartment about a week ago. It was the back part of it that opened to this balcony. The road on the yonder side looked deserted and dark. A solitary streetlight could do nothing much to ward off the darkness of the night. I loved to sit with my cup of coffee in the bedroom adjoining the balcony. As the night became darker, the place increasingly wore a sinister look. I could not understand this. It was as if there were unseen others who wanted to come in. I warded off the uncomfortable feeling, thinking it 'as the play of the mind'. At times, I got up and bolted the door hastily. I felt they were watching me from the adjoining window with glass panels.

I would immediately bolt the other door leading to the dining room. My children did not want to sit in that room to study even during the day, so it became deserted, though we could have put it to good use. Children are in tune with the subtle and can feel a room's energy, though they might not be able to articulate it.

The discussion was soon forgotten, and the rest of my home was always filled with love and laughter, the spiritual and the mundane, as we adjusted to our new environment. We did our prayers every evening, and the GAYANTRI mantra played in the background while we did our tasks. I had had some unique experiences with this powerful mantra earlier.

When I played it continuously for a few hours every day, the house glowed. There was a subtle change in its energies. The sound reverberated around the house and percolated into the dark corners. Even when it was not playing, I could still hear it faintly.

The chant must be done correctly. I use the TIMES MUSIC Gayatri mantra for this. The pause and the ratio of inspiration expiration at different points of the mantra need to be as exact as what has been handed down over the years.

My home now reverberated to an energy that made other lower energies (read ghosts) unwelcome.

Slowly, the unseen slipped out of my mind. Evening prayers became a thing of the past as the number of patients in my clinic increased. I stopped playing the GAYATRI mantra.

My children and I slept together in the bedroom on the front side of the apartment. The front door opened into the sitting room. This bedroom was on the left side of it. The sitting room immediately made its way to the dining room, on the left of which was the kitchen. The dining room, in turn, led to a corridor with two washrooms and a small bedroom yonder. It also led to that room with a balcony. So, I had two rooms that faced the stream. They afforded me bright sunlight throughout the day as they faced the east. This sunlight was welcome as the atmospheric temperature dipped low, especially during the winter.

   I suddenly woke up in the middle of the night one day. It was one a.m. My son was sleeping next to me. My daughter, who was sleeping next to him, was not there. Probably, she had gone to the washroom. Thinking so, I dropped into a slumber. I woke up perhaps after an hour again. My daughter had still not come back! My heart started beating fast. The sound of distant music wafted into my ears.

With a heart that made itself heard, I called out her name. Pitch darkness was around, and I could not see the light switches. Light emerged from below a closed door in the room beyond the washroom. I slowly made my way to the room and pushed the door open.

My daughter was happily talking to someone whom I could not see.

"What are you doing here? Who plays the harmonium in the middle of the night?"

"There is nothing to worry about, Mamma. There is a grandfather here who loves to hear me sing."
"Take leave of him and come to sleep. You must go to school early morning tomorrow."

I bolted the room tight, and we clambered up to bed. I was too tired to dwell on anything at that moment.

I returned before sunset the next day. I must start the evening prayers and the mantra chanting again.
"When did you meet this grandfather for the first time?"
"I think it was more than a month ago. He loves me very much. Do not worry. I have been playing and singing for him every day."

I was overcome with guilt. I had noticed that my daughter looked listless. She dropped off to sleep while studying in the evening. I had thought that the new school and environment were taking their toll. Their father was away in a distant city. He had time to sit back and do nothing with them. They spent hours together, talking, laughing, and rolling about on the bed. They missed his comforting presence.
I never could have that luxury. As I did one chore, the next would wait in line. When I could wrap them up, the children had already slept. Their childhood just passed by me swiftly.

I could not have imagined this as the reason for her listlessness in the wildest of my dreams. Who could it be?
"How does he look? Have you seen him in any photograph before?"
"No, he wears glasses and has loving eyes."
"You look sick because of this lack of sleep. Tell him silently now that you can no longer sing for him

during the night. The neighbours might get disturbed and complain about us. What will we do then? Tell him he can eavesdrop on your music when you practice daily."

She looked down, thinking, and then agreed.

'They are good souls who come visiting at times. There is nothing to worry about.'

My angels informed me. They were always there, speaking to me, warning me, and guiding me, but they never forced me. Whenever I ignored their advice, I suffered and repented later. I have become wiser over time but still faltered at times.

I took a long, soft rope and tied one end to her arm after she slept and the other end to my own. I started playing the mantra again every evening, but as was my wont, I stopped again after a month.

My children had slept early that night. It was past 11 p.m., and I suddenly remembered that my son's school shirt was still outside on the clothesline on the balcony. I was about to open the door when voices started screaming inside me.

'Move away! Do not open the door. He is standing outside.'

My feet trembled, and then the door suddenly dissolved. A tall, hooded man stood outside the door. There were holes in place of his eyes. He wore a long, thick, black, shining coat and shoes. He was smiling.

'Save me, God. Please help.'

I rushed back from the room and bolted the door that led to the dining room. My heart was dancing within me. I ran to the bedroom and dropped into the bed, holding my children tight.

I told my children about it the following day and informed the building owner. My children spoke to their friends, who, in turn, talked to their parents. Many of them had seen him. It was him that the neighbours had been talking about the earlier day.

I could calm down after a few days. The hooded man was searching for peace, and my heart went to him. What could I possibly do to release him from his pain?

I remembered a true story that I had read years ago.
 A lady was travelling by ship. The journey was long, and she wished to go to the vessel's upper deck. The captain, her husband's friend, told her no one could go there.
 Many years ago, one of the sailors had got severely injured. His last dying moments were on that deck. His ghost still roamed about there, looking injured, bleeding and in pain. Anyone who went up there met him.
 She decided to see him. The cabin steward secretly brought her the key. She climbed up the stairs while her heart beat fast. She waited at the door for some time, hearing intently. Only the sea waves lashed...

 The rusted lock took some time to click open. The wind threw open the door. The deck was extended. She walked about slowly, hoping to see him. There was no one. As she turned back, she heard a soft groan.

He stood at a distance from her. One of his eyes was swollen. Blood oozed out from it. His clothes were torn at different places and were soaked in blood. His right arm was twisted at a strange angle. He looked lighter than living human beings who appeared dense. Her hands automatically rose in a blessing. He faded away as she watched.

Back in her cabin, she could not get his image out of his head. She closed her eyes and prayed.
'Please accept your child back, God. He is in so much misery. Relieve him of his pain. Help him.'

Day and night, she prayed for him within her. She continued sending him love and blessings after she reached home, too. Her husband worked for six months on the ship, and then he would be free for the next six months. He helped with her business during that time. She looked forward to that half a year with him.

One night, he told her, "The crewmen consider you a lucky charm. They spend their evenings on that top deck now. They have sent you, their gratitude. How did you do that?"
   Such was her joy upon hearing this that words failed her. Her eyes shone with tears, and her heart bowed in gratitude.
"Thank you so much, God."

 I did the same for days on end. I prayed fervently for his release. I prayed for his beloved girlfriend.

'May they be united again and find bliss together. May all such souls find solace in your kingdom, God. Hold their arms and pull them to you. They have lost their way. Please help them.'

I never met him again. Nor did anyone else in the neighbourhood.

CHAPTER 13

SOJOURN INTO THE PAST

The moment I met my mentor for a course I had registered for, something struck me. What could I not fathom?

Like hundreds of others, I was a student, and he was the teacher. I had yet to learn what he taught us. His enthusiasm and dedication were exemplary, and he cared for each student, painstakingly answering their questions until the dead of the night.
I lagged and could not keep up with others. My mind and life were in disarray. I was recovering from a personal tragedy, and my mind was numb, though I did my professional work to the best of my abilities. But that was all.
I faltered in everything else …

He trusted and believed in me. But a few things amazed me to no end.
I held the last spot among the students but still thought I stood with the mentor. I wished to be of help to him, though I did not know in what way. I saw myself standing beside him, and I could not fathom why.

His voice rang some bells. I heard it in my heart, not with my physical ears. Where had I heard it before? Nevertheless, it made me calm and somehow reset my energies.
  I heard his thoughts clearly and thought he heard mine, too. Many times, he answered my unasked questions. There was a particular frequency match, which made words redundant.

Every time I saw him, I thought he was so fit at all levels, and here I was, so physically and mentally unfit. I wanted to be like him. I told him so once.

I always looked intently at him. His face.... there was something familiar, just outside the reach of my memory. I gazed at his strong arms and thought I was hanging by them.

I felt ashamed of my behaviour at times. The arms you ever hang from are those of your parents as children. He was not one. Why did I think I was clinging to his arm?

You can think of me as crazy. I think so, too, at times. Of course, I cannot always be so. I am an ophthalmologist in a high-profile government organisation, seeing hundreds of patients daily and operating on patients almost daily. I also represent the state at the national level. So, rest assured, I have a head that firmly sits on my shoulders.

I secretly fed off his energy. I could replenish mine when he took live classes. Sometimes, when I felt low, I attended some of his courses for other students to replenish my energies or, shall I say, frequencies. I wrote so once in the telegram group that his students shared. We feed off your energies, and he answered that if it brings good, he is most happy to share them.

Most people are unaware of their energies. Each one of us vibrates to a particular frequency range. When you feel low or have the blues, one of the easiest ways to get out of it is to be near someone who vibrates to a higher frequency. Have you noticed some people whose very presence makes you feel good? Then there are others whose presence for a few minutes makes you feel depleted and low.

Like everything in nature, energy flows from high to low. Those who vibrate in similar frequency ranges are better connected and can quickly replenish each other's energies. Distance is non-existent for them because time and space are relative.

There was a time when I was trying to replenish the energy of a significant other as an experiment. I did not think it amounted to anything. Besides, I had an intense desire to transmit. Suddenly, while doing so, I became so weak that I could hardly move a limb. The truth sunk into my being then.

This is not child's play. Besides, one needs to harness oneself to the Creator, transmit the energy for some time, and stop it consciously. Otherwise, your energy leaks through a pipe you are unaware of throughout the day. As it is, it dribbles as you go about life, meeting various people and facing the day's challenges.

A year passed by. The cool months were approaching. I needed to get my woollens ready.

I was taking out the sweaters when I heard a clear voice. It was the voice of my guardian angel.

'The birthday of a special person is fast approaching.'

My daughter was born on the 18th of October, and she was special.

'It is not about her. It is someone whose birthday falls on the 6th of October.'

I thought hard. No one I knew was born on that day. Who could it be?
'You think who is important in your life as of now.'

There were friends, colleagues, siblings, mentors and my spiritual Guru. I could think of no one else.
The sun shone brightly on October 6th, and the group was flooded with messages. It was my Mentor's birthday.

That day, I was reading a book by the famous Indian author Ruskin Bond. He wrote about the mountains, and I had a strange fascination for them.
   I knew I had lived in a mountainous cave as a hermit in a lifetime. I was a disciple of a GURU and led an ascetic life of prayer, fasting, and meditation. My cave had a stream flowing

through it. I wrapped an orange silk cloth around me as my daily wear at that time.

He wrote about Nand Prayag, the confluence of the River Nandakini with the Alakananda. Many rivers linked up to join either the Ganga or the Jamuna. Someday, I will go there.
I had always wanted to go there...

And then suddenly, it flashed in my mind's eye.

I am among a group of hermits travelling up a mountainous trail. We are all disciples who are going to pay respects to our GURU. All are men, except me. A deep valley runs alongside and falls hundreds of feet below. The trail is brown, narrow, uneven, and full of gravel. The group travels slowly so that I can keep pace. Those in front look back at me, smile and reduce their pace.
 I am so tired that I can no longer walk and collapse on the trail. Walking with me, one turns and says, "Sapna..."
He gives me an arm, and I clamber up.

He is tall, fair, strong, and has almond-shaped eyes. Like me, he is dressed in light orange silk wrapped around him. His right hand has a thick, long stick that helps him climb the mountain. On the other hand, I have a thin, crooked stick that serves little purpose.
   I hang on to his arm as I climb up the long trail. He looks the same as he does now.

He is my mentor. Inadvertently, I still hang by his arm.

CHAPTER 14

NOCTURNAL ADVENTURES

The thunder was deafening. It seemed the sky had turned on all the taps it had. Lying on the bed, I hoped that everyone would remain safe. Half of a house had been washed away the night before, along with two sleeping children downstream. It was only in the morning that the parents came to know about it. My heart could not stop beating hard. The rain had not stopped for more than a week. It still showed no signs of abating.

The polio eradication campaign was going on at the time. There were a few countries where children still had the disease. The government had given strict directives that no child should miss the dose this time. Hectic preparations had been ongoing for a couple of months. The villages were many and scattered, and some were down in the valleys while others were up on the hills. They had one thing in common. Only thirty to forty households made a village. That required many small teams to cover them all. Since there were few staff members, each team worked from the wee hours of the morning.

It was 2.30 a.m. My husband was hurriedly getting ready. He was the leader of his team. My specialisation in ophthalmology afforded me some immunity from fieldwork. My work was routinely in the outpatient departments and the operation theatres. I was glad. When you have little children at home, you cannot leave them at night and go to work.

I brought the water to a boil and then added the grated ginger. It would have to evaporate in half. The fresh tea leaves could then simmer until the water turned pale yellow. A few lemon drops and his tea was ready to be sipped. He liked it this way. I loved my coffee—a tall glass of it.

Outside, the air was still.

"Give me a few packets of salt," he called out. I hurriedly packed the two packets we had in the kitchen, hoping they would suffice. Horns blared through the night.

"They have come," he said and rushed down the stairs.
The road below was illuminated by the lights of two vehicles: a police escort vehicle and a medical van. I watched until the lights disappeared into the night. The road was long and waded through thick jungles up to a point. After that, they would have to walk about five kilometres uphill to a village with no roads. If they did not reach the village before 5 a.m., their mission would fail.

As I scrambled back to the warmth of my bed, my heart ached. The village was a cluster of houses atop a hill. The villagers grew rice in the valleys down below. They would all leave their homes at the break of dawn, leaving their sleeping children behind. They were dead against the idea of giving polio drops to their children.

The disease could only be eradicated once all the children were immunised against it. The police officers served two purposes here. Their presence made the team confident, and they intimidated the innocent villagers into submission. Innocence breeds ignorance.

The bright sun rays streamed in through the glass windows. Birds chirped and flew about in circles in the sky. Some were audacious enough to fly close and chirp into my ears. The sun was indeed shining. The dark-cloaked rain God had made a clear exit. The outdoors and morning chores beckoned at the same time. The latter won. It always did.

It was nearly 10 a.m. by then. I would have to leave for the hospital soon. I wished I could see my husband before leaving. He should have been back by then. As I clambered down the stairs, my eyes fell on him climbing up.

His tired face bled in different places. The white shirt was soaked with large patches of blood. The pants were rolled up to his knees. Lines of blood oozed from his legs and stained the stairs. I was so shocked that no words emerged.

"I fell short of salt. Nothing to worry about," he smiled.

In the washroom, as he sat, I saw the fat leeches stuck to him, sucking blood. They held tight, and I emptied my big table salt container, a spoonful on each of them, till they dropped, wriggling on the floor. They burst bright red when I squashed them. I do not know why I could not stop crying. "I feel no pain," he assured.

Then I saw another one, sucking blood on his neck. I rushed down to my neighbour's house to bring some more salt as my salt container was empty.

Once he was relieved of all of them, he had a bath while I prepared to serve breakfast. The wounds were many, and the antibiotic ointment could hardly cover them all.

"Mission accomplished. We could reach every household and immunise every child. I am happy,"

His enthusiasm was infectious. He could accomplish his mission. But was it wise to throw caution to the winds? Is it not prudent to calculate the risks involved and plan and prepare oneself accordingly? Taking risks can give one a high, and martyrdom can make one a star, but life is precious and given only once.

I, of course, had become wiser. The leeches would not get to suck blood as before. I had packed ten kilograms of salt and an oversized, thick raincoat, complete with a cap, in his backpack.

He would have left for his next mission by the time I returned. My heart was light. All would be well for him this time, as well as for me.

CHAPTER 15

I SLIPPED TO MY DEATH

He looked at me and my hands again. The hands of the sixteen-year-old me were in his big hands. He scrutinised each line on my palm with the most fantastic attention. I sat bewildered. My father sat a little away from me, expecting the verdict.

Mishraji's head was bent low. My mother shuffled in and out between the room and the kitchen. The fries would burn if not watched over.

There was something unique about the man. I could not pinpoint exactly what it was. I thought he was present but not present at the same time. He was physically present, but not all of him was present. That which was absent at that moment had probably gone roaming into faraway galaxies.

Whatever he told me would be gibberish—that I knew for sure. How could astrologers tap into the future? He was a fourth-generation astrologer who kept it under wraps because he was a high-ranking official. In those days, everyone either disbelieved them or, worse, made fun of them. So, he kept his 'science' hidden.

As if astrology was a science, I had secretly scoffed when my father said that an official would come to see me to revisit my future. Yes, it was true. My future had already been visited by a classmate, and it was wrapped in darkness. She read numerology books and had become a self-proclaimed expert. All my friends had deep faith in her. I had accepted her prediction of my doomed future wholeheartedly, as I believed in modern numerology.

She declared, "You will walk to your grave instead of getting a seat in medical school. Stop working so hard."

My parents were mortified to see their studious daughter suddenly sleeping all the time. They were flabbergasted to learn the reason behind it.

"Intense study for years together under the guidance of an adept is needed to become a good astrologer. Teenagers cannot become so by reading a few books," my mother said with a wave.

But I did not believe her. Those were the days when I had great confidence in my beliefs and decisions. Besides, what did my parents know about numerology? My friend was a numerologist and not an astrologer. Their realms were not inclusive of each other — or so I believed.

I was sure my parents were hand in glove with this man and were trying to encourage me with a staged opposite prediction.

"You nearly died as a ten-year-old, didn't you?"

I almost jumped out of my skin. This was my deepest secret. How did he learn it?

My mother had just walked in, and she refuted it strongly.

"Never has such a thing happened."

My father added to the denial vehemently. They then went back to their respective work.

He looked at me, his eyes piercing mine. I nodded, my head bent low while my heart danced as the memories came flooding back.

The road was long, and the bus made the tortuous route up the hill. Filled with boisterous fifth graders, their songs could be heard miles away. They had looked forward eagerly to this once-a-year school picnic and could not stop smiling and laughing. A few lady teachers and a young and athletic guy from the school church, whom we all called 'Brother', accompanied us.

My parents seldom let children travel long distances for picnics and never allowed my siblings this luxury. It was understandable. Those were neither the days of the phone nor the black-tarred roads of today.
But they could not refuse the headmistress who visited us at home, evidently to my great delight, seeking permission to take their 'eldest daughter' to the picnic. She thought that any excursion would be incomplete without me.

We travelled the hills and plains, had lunch by the lake, and pottered around the whole day. Despite strict instructions to the contrary, we spread so far and wide that we could no longer see our teachers. Then suddenly, I found myself alone.

We were atop a flat-topped hill, and the valley fell sharply below. A room was built on the slope's edge, and a few of our things were kept there. I was thirsty and wanted some water.

The front door was accessible through the flat tarred road. I had missed it and saw another door at the back. I slowly descended the hill, which was a bit steep in the upper part. As I climbed down, I could see the depths of the valley.
It was enchanting and held me spellbound. Trucks and dumpers plied about, speeding. They looked even smaller than my toy cars. Colourfully dressed men and women moved about like insects in a canopy of deep green. Wisps of cottony clouds floated above them, slowly moving away. The sky was a brilliant orange-red, and it sent its golden glow down into the valley. Everything deep down was in motion, and I watched transfixed, holding the sill of an open window.

We had been told not to use this door, but it was open and closer, and there was flat mud around it, which I treaded, one step after another. I was lucky that no one was around; otherwise, I would have been scolded severely.
As I put one foot inside the room and tried to balance on the other, I had to let go of the windowsill, and I slipped. But I did not fall. I got up and tried to turn back up, but somehow, I turned towards the valley instead and catapulted downhill. I could not stop, as the valley was steep. It then sharply fell with straight edges thousands of feet below into the toy trucks and insects...

I reached that edge at an incredible speed. My eyes closed in darkness as I hurtled below, but I was stopped in midair.

"Sapna…"
My left hand was yanked by Brother's right hand while his left hand held a lone electric pole.

Slowly, he started pulling me up, but the pole was thick, and he could wrap only half his hand around it. At times, he started slipping himself, and I hurtled down further, but ultimately, he managed to pull me up to his level and then held my hands tightly so we could climb up the hill and reach the flat-topped road.

I was so agitated that I could hardly gulp the water he gave me. He then led me to the bus waiting for us. We were the last ones to file in.

"Where were you? We could not find you anywhere," one of the teachers cried.

"How can you be so irresponsible?" Another said angrily.

"She was with me," Brother said in a way that made them silent.

I could not join the celebrations on the return journey. I sat quietly in the first seat, frightened and shaken. All the others talked and laughed while Brother held one of the stanchions near the seats and stood there, singing, leading all the others. Despite it all, I felt his constant eye on me, watching. When I started to get down from the bus after we reached, he stretched to his full length, still unfurled from holding that stanchion with one hand, and placed his other hand on my head in a blessing.

I was in fifth grade then and met him a few more times in the next two years at that school.

He never said a word but smiled and looked into my eyes, silently enquiring, "Are you well?"

He came to visit all of us on the last day of school. His church duties kept him busy throughout the year, and he was not a teacher. He smiled, held my hands, and wished me luck, but I remember his eyes still full of care and concern.

What is this relationship between the saviour and the saved? The saved gets to live again, and the saviour almost loses his life while saving another. Both are born again at the same time. The relationship formed thus needs no words and has no name, and you need to do nothing to nurture or maintain it. It just exists.

The memories remain hidden forever in some unknown corner, and you can seek respite in them just like that Pole star in the sky, which remains ever present.

So what if you cannot see it all the time?

REVIEW REQUEST

Dear Reader,
Thank you very much for buying and reading this book.

I hope it helps seed your subconscious mind and removes the veil.

We all are divine beings having an experience of human life. Always remember your inherent divinity.

Please do remember to leave a review. It is the LIFELINE of one of the roles I play on this earth, that of an Author.

OTHER BOOKS BY THE AUTHOR

How to BOOST Self-esteem
https://relinks.me/B0CSBNY3CR

How to CREATE Positive Emotions
https://relinks.me/B0D262BVMZ

Workbook on How to CREATE Positive Emotions
https://relinks.me/B0D2VBPW8K

Roses and Thorns Along the Way
A collection of short stories about life
https://relinks.me/B0D27DPWL6

And They Survived
Stories of love, courage, intrigue, and the ultimate triumph of the human spirit
https://relinks.me/B0CW1N659P

How to Transform Negative Emotions
https://relinks.me/B0D42T129Z

DEDICATION

This book is dedicated to my little sister, **Sonali Deb,** a guardian angel who forever bestows love from the heavens. Without her, I could never have embarked on this author's journey.

ACKNOWLEDGEMENT

My heartfelt gratitude goes to my mentor and Lighthouse for this role, Mr Som Bathla.

RIPPED APART

Loud sounds of fury and pain rented the air. Muffled slogans like death knells came closer. "They are coming! Run! Leave everything and run!" Someone was shouting in absolute terror.

Aahana called out to her kids. She ran to the wooden almirah. She would have to pack whatever gold and silver she had and some clothes. Laban, her husband, had been away the whole week. The noise was becoming louder. She would have to run. The neighbours were leaving hurriedly. Her eyes filled with tears. She packed small bundles and gave them to each of the elder two children, Khoka and Babu.
She hoped that Laban was somewhere nearby. He would have known about the grim situation, and she could not afford to wait for him any longer.

"Aahana! Come out fast!" Her friend Shimli was shouting outside the door. She packed the puffed rice into a bundle along with the remaining coconut laddus. The kid's clothes were still drying in the backyard. As she yanked them off the clothesline, she stared in horror as a man was thrown into a burning pyre at a distance. Fearful cries accompanied it. She rushed to the bedroom, grabbed her sleeping daughter, and tied her behind her. Then,

116

holding the hands of her two sons and balancing the other bundles on her head, she rushed out.

A rabid crowd followed. They ran together as fast as they could, and people scrambled to join them. Shortly, they became part of a big crowd. The men and the kids were fast-footed. The women, huffing and puffing with luggage and little kids tied to them, lagged.

A stone gashed right through her feet. In her hurry, she had forgotten to put on her sandals. The brown broken path was lined with weeds and pebbles. The violent mob was slowly closing in.

"Run away! Run away! My feet are giving away. Run as fast as you can," she told her sons.
Her feet were bleeding. She could not walk any longer. They were reluctant.
"Run away. Mingle with that crowd. Some people known to us are there. They will keep you safe. Run now," she said, pushing them away with force.
"Run my dears! Run for your life as fast as you can! If God wills, we will meet again. We will meet again," she hollered after them.

She watched their receding backs as they got smaller and smaller. Then, hiding behind a big clump of bushes, she collapsed into a sea of tears. It was a cloudy day. Black clouds loomed in the distant sky. The mob carried bright, burning wood torches—the village behind burnt red and yellow. The flames leapt in the air. Fearful shrieks emerged as they threw men into the bonfires on the roads. Soon, it would be her turn. She waited, panting and trembling. The child behind her slept peacefully. Hunger had not woken her up.

Each moment, the mob came nearer. She saw a woman being held and her child yanked out and thrown into the fire. Her breasts were slashed off with a sharp sword and tossed aside. A group of men pounced on her.
 Terrified, Aahana crouched a little behind and suddenly slipped into unfathomable darkness.

When she regained consciousness, she found herself in a deep dry well. Dry hay lay below her. Her head was aching. She took in slowly the light filtering in from above. Then suddenly, her heart missed a beat. Her baby! She was still tied to her back. She had fallen on her. She moved and opened the bundle with trembling hands. Why had she not cried until then? How could she, being a mother, fall on her and lose consciousness?

How did her daughter's head slip inside the bundle instead of being out? Please let her be safe, my God.
Oh God! She cried wildly in disbelief and horror. There was no child in it. Only a tiny pillow remained, with two little red flowers embroidered on it. She had left her six-month-

old daughter behind and brought the pillow instead!

She buried her face in her hands and wept uncontrollably.

"Kill me too! Burn me, too! Oh, my dear child, how could I do this to you?" She shouted repeatedly, but her voice was a whimper, and no one heard her.

It was early morning the next day that she felt empty of tears. She had lost everyone—her daughter, her sons, her husband, her house, and everything remotely hers. She was all alone—all alone in the depths of the earth. She laughed out loud and then suddenly stopped. Was she losing her mind?

Dark shadows danced on the walls. Trees and shrubs grew right out of the well. She would hang herself. What use was her life, anyway? Suddenly, her stomach growled. She needed food. Death could wait. She had eaten nothing the earlier day, too. It all started with the sudden announcement of independence and the country's PARTITION.

She rummaged in her bag. The food bundles were with her children. Her bag held only her clothes and that of her little daughter. She covered her face with her daughter's little clothes and wept. Something hard was there in them. She shook them vigorously. Two guavas and a few coconut laddus fell off. She ate them hungrily. It must have been Khoka, her elder son, who had put this in her bag. Her eyes refilled with tears. No, she would not die. They were too small to face the world alone. She would go searching for them and find them. There was no time to lose.

She clutched one shrub and pushed herself up a branch. It held her for some time and then suddenly gave away. She collapsed on the bed of the well below. Getting up again, she jumped and had a thicker branch. Lifting herself slowly, she found her earlier hiding place.

Moving the tall vegetation and shrubs slowly away, she looked around carefully. No one was in sight. She came out cautiously and turned to look back at her village behind. Her feet trembled, and her heart seemed to sink. Only a few houses could be seen. What remained were little stubs emanating smoke. The smoke from their erstwhile bungalow-like house appeared to be the densest. Thick logs were used in its making, and her little daughter combined them, perhaps made it so. Her eyes clouded with tears. She started running as hard as she could, away from it all.

Green fields that stood waving and tall earlier had turned barren. The rice had been harvested and stacked in heaps for the British Sahibs. They had insisted on buying them all. The villagers were not allowed to store some of it for their yearly needs. They were to carry it off in vehicles. The heaps of rice lay smouldering by the roadside instead. At the far end, the Sahibs and their servants were setting fire to the heaps! She went to one heap, took a stick, and moved the burning fire slightly. The husk had burned, but the rice was still warm and good. She dusted the black powder-like husk away and put a handful in her mouth. It didn't taste enjoyable, but it would suffice for her onward journey. She packed as much as she could in her bundle. Some broken coconut shells and a pair of slippers, probably belonging to someone who had fled or was burnt, lay nearby. It fitted her just right. Plucking some banana leaves, she packed them all carefully. Her journey was long, and her destination was unknown. The village had fallen far behind.

She reached the banks of the river Padma. There was a makeshift police station and some tents. Rushing towards them, she anxiously searched for a familiar face. Little boys were running around, but although she had carefully scanned their faces, none were hers. She went to the British man sitting in the main room. His face brightened up when she spoke in English. She anxiously asked about her kid's whereabouts. He scanned the register and shook his head.
"They probably did not come in to register their names. The violent mob was not far away; most moved away as quickly as possible. We are understaffed," he mumbled.

"Did all of them move away yesterday itself?" She asked.

"Yes. Those here have arrived this morning," he said.

There was a horn from a big ship. She ran towards it and climbed in just before it left. It was overcrowded. A man moved away on seeing her, giving her space to sit. She smiled at him.
The ship moved and then picked up speed. The receding shores of her motherland slowly became fainter. All that was dear was lost forever.

The water made a strange sound as if boring into her, carving out her grief and dissolving it within itself. The sun turned the water red and orange, reflecting it on her face. The cool air dried up her tears. She felt light and relaxed. Someone was distributing small paper packets. People ate the puree and potato curry in it hungrily.

"Who is making these arrangements?" One of them asked.
"Abdul Mia is the owner of the small boats. He has spent a fortune trying to serve those who have lost everything. His makeshift kitchen is near the shore. He and his family members make these day and night. His two teenaged sons come running with these, to each leaving ship," one man said.

A few hands rose in a blessing. Aahana watched the contented faces with solace in her heart. She had eaten two purees and packed the rest in her bundle.

The mind has wings. It flew to her parenteral house. They were a huge joint family. All the relatives stayed together. She had thirty cousin brothers and nineteen cousin sisters. The latter were all married off at an early age. She hardly remembered them and grew up mainly with the boys. She was close to two of her cousins, Khokon and Santosh. She went running, hunting, fishing, and horse riding with them.

They got up early in the morning for running. Her father was the second of the brothers, and his knowledge and wit made him a favourite among the children. He was a strict disciplinarian. The children accompanied him with their neem twig brushes every morning. They hurried or ran, for their uncle had their path chalked out clearly in his head. He had to supervise a large estate and check on the vast fields and the lakes called as 'Pukoors'. He sent a few elder boys to collect the milk and milk items from the byre. Others went to bring back vegetables from the farm. They were given this duty in turn, for each got their favourite vegetables back, completely ignoring the choice of others!

The family owned hundreds of cows, buffaloes, and goats. Near far away from their shed stood the houses of those who worked in the estate. Chacha Sabir oversaw the day-to-day working of the byre. 'Chana', better known as paneer, butter and ghee, was made of different milk varieties. They would be neatly packed and labelled in Bengali. Many women in the house did not touch buffalo milk or its ghee and patronised only the cow's milk and ghee. Two of her grandmothers lived only on goat's milk throughout the day. Aahana found them strange. She thought they were as bad as the kids. They ate nothing else but still were strong and did not need the stick. She thought it was incredible.

She loved the granular sweet-smelling ghee made of buffalo milk the best, and though most of it was turned into paneer and ghee to be distributed to the workers of the byre, Chacha Sabir always kept a glass bottle filled with the golden fluid, especially for her. She never told her father of this. He believed eating ghee of buffaloes would make her lazy, and Cow's ghee would make her elegant and light-footed instead. She thought she was light-footed enough already.

She would often leave all the others and sneak into Sabir Chacha's house. They had dogs, cats, and goats of their own. His two daughters, Samina and Sabrina, were nearly her age. They played together. Chachi gave them hot, steaming rice, ghee, and freshly fried crisp fish. She loved it. Even the hot mung dal and big brinjal slices fried to a rich dark brown colour with a melt-in-the-mouth texture tasted heavenly in their house.

Her stomach growled in happy anticipation. She drank a few sips of water. She would have to learn to ignore the hunger pangs and make whatever food she had last for a long time.

Huge pots boiled one after another in a long row by massive wood fires. One had lentils, and a few others had rice and vegetables. The servants ground mustard in big grinding stones along with green chillies, turning it into a paste. Once the water in the pot started boiling, they would send the elder brothers fishing in one of the twenty-seven lakes in their estate. The freshly caught fish would then be cut, cleaned, washed, and dropped into the boiling mustard pot. Fresh coriander leaves cut in heaps would be put in before they brought the pot down. The man servants did the latter. She watched the ladies of the house doing all this with machine-like precision, enchanted. Her father would call her if he saw her doing this too often.

"You will do this and more when you grow up. Go to the study room and sit with your brothers. Listen to the teachers carefully. You must know the languages well, especially Bengali and Sanskrit. Do not ignore your English and Mathematics lessons. You will need all this later in your life," he would tell her lovingly.

Her mother scoffed at all this.

"You are a girl and should behave like one. After all, you will get married and do what I do every day of your life," she would tell her sternly.

She would teach her sewing, mending, cutting vegetables, cooking, and serving.

An apple in everyone's eye, she reigned like a queen in their hearts. Her quick wit and intelligence impressed their English teacher, Mr. Anderson. She reminded him of his little daughter, who was home in England. He told her about his country, the rivers, snowfall, and autumn. One day, he would take her there with her father's permission. She could then see it herself.

She spoke to him about the lakes, birds, and the orchard. The giant watermelons, which afforded her an excellent hiding place while playing hide and seek, surprised him no end. The mangoes were the juiciest best in the place. But as much as she wanted, she could never take him to see all that. Her father strictly discouraged 'outsiders' from entering the house's interiors or fields. How could a man continue to be an outsider for so many years? Her father was difficult to understand.

Then came the news of his transfer to a school far away. She was heartbroken. Consoling her, he gifted her a beautiful foreign doll when he left. It remained with her till she got married. She gave him a soft, thick shawl on which she had embroidered a golden flying Eagle. Her son's sweaters had the same design on the back. It suddenly seemed that the eagles had turned real and flown away.

Khoka and Babu repeatedly turned to look at their mother's face. How could she tell them to run away, leaving her? The mob inched closer to them. They ran as fast as they could, mingling with the crowd, rushing away. They were going towards the river. On the shore stood a few small boats and ships. They seemed overcrowded. Where would they go? Whom did they have on the other side? They sat below a tree and watched people falling over each other to climb into them. They would wait for their mother. The banyan tree was huge and a little away from the shore. They climbed on it and hid comfortably. They saw the mob with flames inching nearer. Would they search the tree? They trembled with fear. Instead of coming towards the river, the mob turned towards another village. They heaved a sigh of relief.

 They waited all day, but their mother did not come. The waters were turning orange by the setting rays of the Sun. Far away, they could see their village burning a similar colour. Turning towards the shore, they saw only two ships remaining. Few people were still standing there, perhaps waiting for someone. Children held their father's hands and climbed onto the ship. It reminded them of their father. He had left the house about a week before, kissing them goodbye in the night's dark, promising to return once his secret mission was complete. Though they always saw him infrequently and for a short duration, his love for them was always abundant.

Their mother had raised them alone. She managed the farms, orchards, rice fields, and workers. Now, they had nothing left. Their whole village had been turned into ashes.

If only they could see their father one last time...

"Khoka ... Babu..." Someone called out just then.

Read the rest of the story in...

AND THEY SURVIVED

AFTERWORD

I have had a strange childhood. Ironically, it seems odd retrospectively, for while I was amid it, it seemed perfectly normal.

Born more than half a century ago, I remember the doctors who came to visit me eagerly every morning at different times, blaming their busy routine for it. One had a black dot mark on her face, and they delighted in me. I had quite an active mind, for I was only a few days old then, but I still wondered at their liking for me.

I was bored of being locked in that little frail body and did not give it much thought or respect. I was so tired of that body that I sailed about the room.

That sailing body of mine was light, and instead of legs, there was a tapering end. I sat on the headstand of one bed and then the other and did not quite like those white beds placed so close to each other and the number of people in that room.

I remember that months after I was born, my spirit used to hang around outside, and my mother used to carry my live body. I say 'live' to not confuse you, my dear reader. You might imagine me dead by the description I am presenting.

While she carried me about, I just floated beside her, getting tired at times of all that floating.

Once, my body was very sick, and my mother was walking sadly, thinking that I might die.

I was listening to her and thinking that I did not care if that body died. I was tired of hanging around it anyway!

When I got attached to that body, I cannot say but I still hang loose, even after all these years on this planet.
Since these are unrealistic and shocking revelations, I will not immediately unfurl all this on you.

But this courage did not come easy. For years, I hid behind silence, trying to blend in, even when I was singularly different and afraid to reveal what I saw and knew so well.

Was I doing a disservice to the world by keeping what I saw under wraps?

My eyes fell on a piece of advice a few years back during my esoteric studies. (I had to seek answers to keep my senses intact)

It said, "Reveal to The World What Is Revealed unto You."

So, shall I do...

I shall reveal slowly in my books. The stories are surprising, scary, and touching.
But isn't life itself like that?

Printed in Great Britain
by Amazon